# REFERRALS
# The Professional Way

## 10 Strategies for Networking with High-Net-Worth Clients & Centers of Influence

BY

FRANK MASELLI, CIMC

# Referrals: The Professional Way

## 10 Strategies for Networking with High-Net-Worth Clients & Centers of Influence

The Frank Maselli Company
9 Cranberry Drive
Franklin, MA 02038
800-283-1155
www.frankmaselli.com

Printed and bound in the United States of America

ISBN: 1-59971-182-6

Other books by Frank Maselli

**_Seminars: The Emotional Dynamic (2<sup>nd</sup> Edition)_**

This book is dedicated with love to my wonderful wife
Rebecca Cole Maselli
and my two amazing daughters
Gerilyn and Rachel.

❊ ❊ ❊

To you…the professional financial advisors
who work so hard for your clients every day.

❊ ❊ ❊

To the courageous men and women of our armed forces and
their amazing families.
They are at war for our way of life and I am humbled by their
selfless sacrifice.

# Preface

Twice, early in my career, I was nearly out of this business. The second time, I came within a single day of quitting and going to work a construction job in New York City if you can even believe that! How my life would have been different is impossible and frightening to imagine.

We all have our moments of triumph and despair. I have certainly known more than my share of triumph and I meet with advisors every day who are having more fun and success than they could have imagined. But I believe many others are struggling and I want to help.

Growing a business is harder today than it has ever been before, but the rewards are worth the effort, so I'm very glad you are reading this book. I hope it makes a positive difference in your practice and your life.

I could never have written this book without the tremendous support and patience of my wife Rebecca. She encouraged me all the way and kept me focused whenever I started to wander off course. There is no way to tally up the immense cost of the weekends and evenings spent at the keyboard. But somehow my account always balances with her.

Kara Lee McCormick is my editor and I am indebted to her for adding a professional touch to this effort. Her skill is extraordinary and she took this work over the goal line. What a great partner!

It's a bit self-serving to thank your boss, but I'll take the risk. John Hailer is the President and CEO of IXIS Asset Management Advisors Group. He is a man with a powerful vision and philosophy of how things can be done in this industry. He put together an extraordinary team and created a culture of trust, empowerment and fun unlike anything I've ever seen before. Time will tell, but slowly, this company is becoming a force for change in this business. I'm excited and proud to be part of it.

Thanks always to my friend and mentor Bob Donato who taught me as a manager to always respect and fight for my advisors.

Finally, to my two top advisors...Nick Murray and Dan Sullivan! Every idea that emerges from these men is a symphony of logic, humor, inspiration, wisdom and passion. Whichever course you chart through this crazy business...you couldn't choose better guides. They are brilliant beacons in this storm of confusion.

# TABLE OF CONTENTS

# Part 1
# The Set-Up

*Chapter 1*

# Time For A Change!

$A$nyone who tells you that getting referrals from top clients is as easy as simply *asking* for them either doesn't really *have* any top clients or is using way too many recreational pharmaceuticals.

This book will teach you a new philosophy and a set of simple strategies for generating referrals that actually taps into the most advanced thinking about high-net-worth clients. We are going to equip you with skills that will enable you to open up the world of connections surrounding your very best clients and centers of influence, like accountants, attorneys and business managers. Whether you're a raw rookie or a seasoned professional, you can use these strategies to create a referral-based practice starting immediately.

*For the sake of simplicity in reading this book, whenever you see the phrase "HNW client," just assume that it also means CPAs, estate attorneys, business managers, and all other potential centers of influence who might have clients that would benefit from your expertise. These professionals are special people with whom we can build mutually rewarding referral relationships. They have most of the same fears and concerns about referrals as high-net-worth clients, so the same basic rules apply to all groups with only a few slight variations, which I will detail for you.*

The ideas in this book are powerful, but simple and easy to use. They do not require an advanced knowledge of psychology to apply. Yes, we will be talking about the mind of the client and about their attitudes toward us and the referral process, but these are mostly common-sense observations that anyone who works with people can see for themselves.

Most important, you are going to learn techniques that are based on real-world client and advisor behavior...not on wishful thinking about how people *should* react. These ideas have been "field tested" for many years. They come from my personal use as well as from two decades of direct study of top advisors in action. So they work and they *will* work for you if you use them.

## Referral frustration?

If you've ever been frustrated because you know you need to get more referrals and you know your clients are happy with you and you *deserve* referrals but you don't feel armed with the right words or techniques...hope has arrived. By the end of this book, you will be ready to build the kind of business you have always wanted...a thriving, growing financial practice that reaches out proactively and helps great people succeed.

I ask only one thing: take your time, start at the beginning and let the lessons unfold at their natural pace. Some of you will want to skim around the chapters and pick out ideas at random, and that can work, but it's less effective than getting the full picture first. Everything ties together here.

Referrals are a process, not a snapshot magic conversation. It has taken our industry a long time to get the referral concept as messed up as it is today. You have probably learned a career's worth of bad techniques and there is quite a bit of "de-programming" required to clear your head. A few hours and a little patience will get you going in the right direction for the rest of your life, and it will be well worth the effort.

As Dan Sullivan, founder of The Strategic Coach, is fond of saying, *"No progress can be made until the truth is told."* The overarching truth in our industry that we've been fighting for decades to hide is...

## Referrals are not easy

Referrals are very tricky things that touch on a wide variety of human emotions and psychological issues. The old techniques you've been taught (and are *still* being taught) do not work with today's more sophisticated clients…and using them may be hurting you in ways you cannot imagine.

These backward and ineffective approaches are mostly based on the way someone thinks clients *should* behave in theory…not in the reality of the HNW client in our industry today. That can be seen in popular phrases that many advisors use or *try* to use every day. Brilliant tactics like:

> *"So…who else do you know who might be interested in this idea?"*
>
> *"I need your help to grow my business, Bob."*
>
> *"I get paid two ways."*
>
> *"If you were me, Bob, how would you penetrate the physician community?"*
>
> *"May I have your permission to brainstorm a bit?"*
>
> *"If you like me…don't keep me a secret!"*
>
> *"I expect all my clients to give me referrals."*

Or that great piece of Zen claptrap: *"Ask by not asking."* What the hell is that?

Folks, if you use these techniques with HNW clients, I can almost guarantee you they are thinking "Loser" with a capital L, or worse…SALESMAN!

## *Not the techniques…you!*

The fascinating and scary thing is some of you may be using these techniques and actually having some success at getting referrals.

Ironically, you're not getting the referrals *because* of these techniques, but in spite of them. The techniques are terrible! They always were and they always will be terrible! It's YOU that's good. You have an abundance of natural charm, charisma or personal style that engenders trust in the mind of your clients. You're so good in fact that you've somehow managed to transcend a bad technique. How much more successful could you be if you took all that "trust-ability" and paired it up with a more powerful and intelligent referral process? Your results would be incredible!

Ten or twenty years ago in our industry, a good rap was all you needed. That sharply honed "salesman patter" was the ticket to a successful business. But clients have changed. They have become jaded by a decade of bombardment by the media about how we cannot be trusted. Our industry has done a pretty good job of undermining its own credibility at times even without the media's help. Given this new reality, I say it's time to end that slick approach to referrals.

No longer will you come off like the pushy, used-car salesman twisting the arm of a good client for a few names. Referrals will be a natural and comfortable part of your everyday conversations.

Those of you who read my book, *Seminars: The Emotional Dynamic* may recall how we redefined the presentation process by looking at seminars from the audience's perspective. We dissected the *Nine Critical Emotions* that made a super-effective presentation. I want to do the same thing with referrals.

We're going to break down the referral process and rebuild it with a more detailed and psychologically informed understanding of what makes top clients and prospects tick. I believe that only by doing that can you take your business where it needs to go.

## We need referral help

We seem to have a very big disconnect in this industry when it comes to referrals. According to Horsesmouth.com (the great information website for financial professionals), referrals are by far the hottest topic on the site. More than 80% of respondents to their survey said that the inability to ask for referrals was the number one gap in their business.

And the gap isn't a new phenomenon. I recall seeing an industry survey many years ago that said more than 90% of financial advisors claim referrals are critical to their success, yet 75% said they **never** ask for referrals. Both of those studies confirm my own experiences and observations of advisor behavior over the past two decades and I think I figured out why this disconnect exists.

### Referrals take trust...and trust must be earned!

In your heart you *know* this. As a sensitive, intelligent human being you understand the concept of trust proved over time in a relationship. Yet many of the old referral techniques ignore this reality and force us to push our hard-won client relationships faster and further than we know or *feel* they're ready to go.

What's worse is that all those clever phrases and sales tricks we've been taught actually create *anti-trust* and so most of us have decided not to use them. We're too smart for the old ways, but we've had nothing to replace them with...until now.

To master the process of referrals we must first understand a little about trust.

## Three levels of trust

Trust, like love or fear, is a highly complex human emotion. So why should we assume that all trust is the same and that all relationships experience trust at the same pace? It's not a uniform, one-dimensional thing, but a thickly layered and lumpy emotional concept, like a big piece of lasagna.

The three main layers of trust in our world are:

### Level one: *"I trust you with some of my money."*

This is where a prospect makes the decision to open an account and begin a relationship with you. Everyone knows it's rare that a top client gives you all their money on day one. They may be testing you out with a portion of their total portfolio or trying an idea or two that you've recommended. Referrals do not take place on level one.

On level one, much of the prospect's decision to work with you is sort of a leap of faith in a way. They may like you on a superficial level. They may like your idea...even though they don't fully comprehend it. They also base much of this initial decision on the quality of your firm. So companies spend big bucks on branding messages, products and processes — all of which are supposed to enhance your credibility with the client.

If you're independent, you're not really able to take advantage of company trust and branding. So you rely more on the prospect's inherent mistrust of Wall Street. You sell the concept of independence and customized thinking...which is its own type of trust and brand.

### Level two: *"I trust you with my wealth!"*

This is where the client begins to open up and relies more completely on your advice. No longer do they say things like, *"Send me something on that idea will you?"* or *"Let me think about that!"* They do what you tell them because they finally figured out that you know what you're doing and have their best interests at heart.

On level two, they are buying more into you. They are having experiences with you and these collectively increase or decrease trust over time. Some clients stay forever at level two. You can have a great, long-term relationship right here, and you think that referrals should happen at this point but they don't. There is actually another level with HNW clients…a higher plateau that you rarely get to visit. Referrals take more than a very happy client.

### Level three: *"I trust you with my friends, family, colleagues and critical relationships!"*

At this level, a client says to himself, "I know you, believe in you, have confidence in your ideas, but beyond that — I like and respect you personally and professionally. You take good care of me and have proved reliable. Your style is appealing and you fit in as a critical part of my world. I am now willing to introduce you to others in that world — my friends and important personal relationships."

This is the HNW Referral Zone. At level three, the firm and the product are far less important than you. Referrals, in fact, are all about you. HNW clients don't generally refer someone to a company. They almost never refer someone to a product. Instead they refer to a specific person...in this case you, to whom they have bonded at this critical third level.

## That's too much time!

*"How long will it take to get to the level three trust referral stage with a good client? I don't have years to wait for all this trust to build up. I want to get started today!"*

The good news is that the process of developing referral-generating trust can be accelerated and catalyzed through the application of intelligent, psychologically informed principles that we will discuss. You can actually start building a referrals-based practice today — even on day one with a totally new client!

You will also learn how to relax and enjoy the referral conversation. Life is too short and this business is too stressful to force yourself to do things you hate or that cause you pain when you do them. In fact, pain is a pretty good indicator that you're doing something wrong. Referrals can actually be fun and they can position you from strength...not weakness. They don't need to be the back and forth battle of wills we have seen for years:

### – Advisor

*So who else do you know who might be interested in this idea?*

### – Client

*Gee, I really can't think of anyone.*

### – Advisor

*Well then...do you mind if we brainstorm a bit? How about your doctor, your lawyer, your business partner?*

### – Client

*No...I'm pretty sure they already have advisors and brokers.*

### – Advisor

*Well, most of my best clients have several financial advisors. After all, no one has a monopoly on good ideas.*

### – Client

*You know...I really don't like to get involved in my friends' finances.*

### – Advisor

*Well I get paid two ways.*

Haven't we had enough of this surreal sales crap? You simply cannot wrestle with HNW, successful, intelligent clients. Well, you *can* but why would you *want* to? Is this the way *you* would like to be approached by an advisor in your world? Of course not.

You will learn several key ideas based on simple human understanding. They are part science and part art and together they will allow you to build a massive business without ever resorting to clever conversational combat.

The battle is over!

## A broken process

The entire referral process in our industry is badly damaged if not crippled beyond repair. At a time when millions of investors are in desperate need of quality advice — many struggling to retire or reach the most fundamental financial goals — we sit unwilling or unable to reach out and ask for referrals to help them. Surely that's a sign of a bad process.

If you assume that most advisors want to help people (which I do) and if you also assume that given a way to reach out to *more* people most advisors would use it (which I also do)…then you must conclude that it's the techniques themselves that are at fault and not some massive systemic failure of advisor psyche. In simplest terms…we care and we're not lazy…so it must be something else.

When I came into this business, people told me, *"Clients are eager to refer you. All you have to do is ask them for names!"* I heard this everywhere…from managers, top producers, consultants and those ubiquitous mass-market, self-help sales gurus like Joe Girard, Brian Tracy, Tony Robbins, Tom Hopkins, and others.

After working under that philosophy and failing miserably, I thought it was my fault. I was semi-convinced that I just didn't have the courage to be successful. I wasn't bold enough or dynamic enough to be a top salesman.

I tried hard to do what they told me, but the words and the techniques bothered me. I'm not sure why. I never had any formal training in psychology or advanced sales skills when I entered the business. There was just something in my head that told me *"this is wrong"* whenever I tried the things I was taught.

Yet I saw these supposedly great advisors who seemed to have this cold-blooded, business-building streak and I envied them. It seemed that they would let nothing stand in the way of their success. They pushed harder, asked for more, and reaped the early rewards of that boldness. *"Why can't I be like them?"* I wondered. But I couldn't do it and it ate away at me until I found that many of my colleagues felt the same way.

In fact, as I dug deeper I started to notice that very few of my colleagues were *using* these techniques at all. It was some kind of sham! It turned out that several of those "Superstars On Parade" had some other secret of success, like an inherited book, a couple of huge institutional accounts, or a girlfriend who worked at a bank and was funneling them lists of clients with maturing CDs.

To make it more confusing, the really great advisors who *did* have exceptional client skills were actually very client-sensitive and professional about referrals. They weren't using the aggressive, old-school techniques either.

That's when it dawned on me that the real path to success might be different from what I had learned. It could be observed by studying and watching great advisors but they were generally *not* the people doing the sales training. In fact, top practitioners rarely talked about how they did things. They were rather quiet about their skills and techniques partly out of a desire to preserve their success but mostly because they knew that everyone must find their own path.

Lessons learned on your own are more valuable and permanent than lessons passed on by others. Success must be earned! Great advice given before the recipient is professionally ready to receive it is often wasted. It is only through years of careful observation of many of these top pros backed up with actual trial and error that I arrived at my own approach.

That said, the lessons in this book may not help you at all unless you actually try the ideas for yourself and customize them to fit your style. You cannot learn without doing! Some things you may use verbatim, but most will need your personal touch. Your experience will be different, perhaps even better, than mine. And then you'll write your own book and the circle will be complete.

## *Only for 10%*

The concepts in this book are mainly directed at the top 10% of your client base. They will work for anyone, but for most of your clients, this may be overkill. Many of your clients will probably give you referrals no matter *what* technique you use. They like you and are happy with your service…so go ahead and ask them in any way you want and you will probably get some names.

The problem is that you don't really *want* referrals from everyone. Referrals are not intended as a mass marketing strategy. They are the ultimate rifle shot target marketing approach. And besides, you simply cannot help everyone. Most people don't need the sophistication or intensity of advice and service you deliver.

The clients you really want referrals from are a select group of successful, high-net-worth, influential people who can truly benefit from your skill and can put you in touch with VERY big money. If you look hard, you may have only ten or fifteen of them in your book. So it's a small group we're dealing with here.

You know who these folks are. They are the ones who could change your entire world with a few well-placed phone calls. I've seen it happen and it's amazing! These are the movers and shakers — the people who could gain you access to $50, $100, $500 million in net new assets if they really opened up their world to you in a meaningful way and hand-carried you around to meet friends and colleagues.

It's often easy to build great relationships with these folks because they are wonderful people, but it's also very difficult to ask them for referrals. The irony is that you're reluctant to ask them for referrals precisely *because* you like having them as great clients and you don't want to screw that up.

You may have thought, *"Hey I'm lucky to have you and if I push you for referrals you may think that I'm not as grateful as I should be."* I'm telling you it's a convoluted emotional world inside these heads of ours.

For these folks, the act of referring involves a complex set of social and professional interactions that carry tons of risk for them. It often forces them to involve themselves in your world or in the world of a friend or colleague to a far greater extent than they ever want to or have time to do.

Getting them to open up takes skill, subtlety, intelligence, sensitivity and awareness on your part — the exact opposite of everything you've been taught about referrals…until now.

## No perfect approach

There is no one perfect strategy or magic referral phrase that works all the time and with every client. I wish there were...that would make everything so easy. Searching in vain for that "silver bullet" has been part of our industry's problem for decades.

Referrals are a career-long process that unfolds at a pace determined by your ability and the quality of the relationships you have with your clients. Those relationships, in turn, are driven by many variables, only a handful of which are under your control.

You need to professionalize your various referral approaches to match different clients and different scenarios and to accelerate that "life-long" part down to a more manageable time-frame that will help you grow your business.

## Really...how bad are the old ways?

Pretty horrible actually — so bad, in fact, that they risk your relationships with your best clients. They are conversationally awkward and uncomfortable both for the client and for you. They place you in a very bad or weak position with the exact person to whom you need to appear strong and confident.

### Bad timing

Bad timing is part of the problem. Many advisors are still being taught to ask for referrals at the very start of the relationship — long before they have had a chance to build rapport or earn trust in any way.

You *can* bring up the subject of referrals on day one...we're going to learn how. But to aggressively ask for referrals at the moment you "close" the business is a psychologically misaligned strategy that should never be used with your top ten clients.

Picture this: The client has just agreed to your portfolio proposal. They've signed the new account form and are sliding the check across the desk in your direction. And now you're supposed to say:

> *"So tell me Bob, who else do you know who might be interested in this kind of program?"*

The emotional dissonance that you've just created here is staggering. First, the act of signing the check or agreeing to do business creates a significant moment of buyer's remorse. There's always a few seconds of internal uncertainty that comes with every financial decision no matter how confident people seem on the outside.

So now you've been taught to take that moment of remorse and make it even *more* uncomfortable by asking for names of friends and colleagues. All this does is increase the uncertainty. The client finds themselves thinking... *"Oh my god what did I just do? Who is this guy? Why is he asking me about my friends? Does he really care about me or was that whole thing an act just to get my money? Here we go...another typical salesman. I made a mistake and I want my check back!"*

Push too hard too soon for referrals with a HNW client and that emotional misstep could cost you a lifetime of connections that might have permanently improved the landscape of your world.

## Looking weak

When the client looks into your eyes, they want to see a reflection of themselves. They want to feel important, strong, intelligent, successful and in command. If the way in which you ask for referrals makes you look weak, hesitant or desperate, they will begin to question their decision to work with you. Go too far and they may even begin to resent you for making them feel bad about themselves.

Many popular referral techniques send precisely the wrong subliminal messages about the health and strength of your business. They make you look like a hollow-cheeked waif in a Charles Dickens novel struggling to survive.

*"Please sir...I need some more names!"*

Hey, we all struggle at some point in our careers...that's no big secret. But transmitting a feeling of deprivation and need would be the exact wrong way to gain the trust of a top client.

## *Superman*

There are some people who can make these old techniques work. They came to Earth with powers and abilities far beyond those of mortal man. People blessed with extraordinary personalities who can rip out your spleen with a rusty butter knife and make you feel like you were strolling on a beach in Anguilla with Nicole Kidman.

I actually met an advisor with that kind of personality at a conference a few years ago. He was teaching a class on referrals and all his techniques were these old-school, clumsy, oppressive and psychologically uninformed ones that I'm telling you not to do. It was so bad I started to get physically sick.

But I forced myself to listen harder mostly out of sociological curiosity. Slowly, surprisingly, something began to change. This guy was actually pretty funny, engaging, self-effacing and entertaining. In fact, by the end of his talk I found myself really liking him despite his absurd techniques. I could actually see where a client might become enthralled and want to give him referrals. It was amazing. He just had the kind of personal charm and sense of humor that made all his stupid techniques work...for him. Yet as fascinating as it was to watch...I wondered what kind of superstar he could really become with some advanced skills.

I'm not Superman. I need some referral skills that actually help, not hurt. But if the old ways are still working well for you then simply take a few new ideas from this book that make sense and augment your current approach. My guess is that you will see improved results.

## *Who should be reading this book?*

I think the concepts in this book would be helpful to a very wide audience of professionals, but the examples and the terminology are geared toward the financial advisor, stockbroker, financial planner, investment consultant, wealth manager, registered rep, insurance agent, wholesaler, and manager.

However, you may know people who work with wealthy clients like attorneys, accountants, business managers, luxury car dealers, bespoke clothing salespeople, business coaches, pharmaceutical reps, and advertising executives. Feel free to tell them about the book. They would probably appreciate it and maybe even send you a few referrals. At least the ideas in the book would demonstrate to them how seriously and professionally you *take* referrals...so you're elevating your stature in their minds. How many of you realized that's a great idea? If you did...congratulations! You just passed the first test.

## *Lots of ideas*

I know that many of you have probably attended some kind of referral training in the recent past. Maybe your firm hired some "guru" to come in and change your world. I've heard stories about what others are teaching out there and I totally respect their opinions.

My goal is not to conflict with any of the other referral "experts." In fact, many of our ideas may be complementary. This book is not intended to be a collection of best practice ideas on referrals. Based on what I've seen, that's often like the blind leading the blind.

The ideas in this book come entirely from my own experiences and observations. So if something you read in here agrees with another idea you've heard from another expert, then that idea may have extra validity because it means the two of us came up with it independently.

All of that is a long-winded way of saying that no one person or firm has the corner on the best referral approach. Learn from everyone and apply all of this knowledge to your world. Take what fits your personal style and discard the rest. It's a buffet of ideas and you get to pick whatever works for you. In any true science, a theory must be tested and proved with repeatable results to be valid. You are urged to do so.

*Chapter 2*

# Why Referrals?

The first question is: "Why do you want referrals?" and the number one answer is...

## *Because you care!*

Deep down, referrals are *not* about you growing your business, although that is one of the tremendous side benefits of a strong and effective referral process.

Referrals *are* about you wanting to help more people avoid their biggest fears and fulfill their grandest dreams through the application of sound and professional financial advisory skill.

We are going to explore this philosophical shift further in a while, but if you think referrals are just another asset-gathering, business-building tool like cold calling or direct mail...you're going to miss one of the main themes in the new era of financial services — the fact that we have transitioned (albeit with much pain and not completely yet) from a sales to a service profession.

Putting referrals in this new perspective allows you to tap into the most powerful energy source in our world — the biggest, strongest success driver in our business — the desire to take great care of people!

So the first reason you want referrals is because you're really gifted at what you do and you want to share that quality advice with the most important people in your world. This is true whether you are a raw rookie or multi-decade advisor. Now we can discuss the mechanics of referrals as a business strategy.

## They are more professional

Referrals carry an upscale feeling and prestige appropriate to a seasoned, successful practitioner in any arena. Compared to many of the marketing techniques that we use to reach out to new clients, referrals are one of the most professional. Even if you are new to the business, referrals lend an air of credibility to your efforts. They make you seem more serious and credible.

All professionals get referrals — accountants, attorneys, doctors. In fact, top clients are generally very comfortable with the concept of referrals as something that true professionals do. So it's not like you're going to be hitting them with some alien idea they've never experienced. They will know how to react.

One problem is that top clients react to us differently than they would to a doctor or accountant. That's because many still think of us as salespeople and somehow less professional than doctors and lawyers. That's wrong, but it's a deeply ingrained idea that only dissipates as they come to know you better in the relationship.

## It replaces traditional prospecting

For many top advisors, referrals may be the main if not only source of new clients. We all know that we should never stop prospecting, but when you get to a certain point in your career, handling more clients and more assets, prospecting usually gets put on the back burner. This is dangerous because things like market action and attrition can eat away at your asset base. Referrals can counterbalance those forces.

Even if you are a rookie, you want to send a message that says referrals are the main way in which you accept new clients. This makes you seem selective and careful about growing your practice. It creates a feeling of exclusivity that appeals to the HNW client. If you're taking every Tom, Dick and Mary that walks in the door with two nickels to rub together, they might ask... *"Why am I working with you? Where's the prestige?"* The idea that... *"My advisor doesn't work with just anyone"* makes *them* feel more important.

## They're already sold on you

The referral is predisposed to like you before you say a word. Your client has told their friend or colleague what a great person you are, consequently, there's a bit of love built into the new relationship right from the start. You have less self-selling to do and can focus more on the new client.

A referred prospect is usually more willing to open up and discuss their situation than someone you acquire in other ways. They may be more ready to accept your ideas because they conclude that if you are handling money for their trusted friend or colleague, you must know what you're doing. Bang...the relationship gets off to a stronger start!

This is good because it frees you up to concentrate on understanding the client and building trust rather then proving you know the difference between a stock and a bond.

## The "Look-Alike Principle"

Referrals enable you to capture a similar demographic and psychographic group as your best clients. You've heard the old adage *"Birds of a feather flock together."* Well, it's true. You have a high-net-worth client...maybe a successful business owner who lives in a nice neighborhood and has a lot of money to invest. Guess who they hang around with? The same basic type of people. This can help you network and eventually synergize the growth of your business into target niches.

But the "Look-Alike Principle" can also work in reverse if you're not careful. You have a few clients from whom you might not *want* referrals. *"Please...no more like you!"* These are the P.I.T.A. clients. Pain In The @$$! As financial industry guru Nick Murray might add, *"I say that with love."*

The good news is that with referrals, you get to decide the types of people you want to do business with by carefully selecting the clients you want to "clone." This means that referrals are a way for you to take control of your business and drive it where *you* want it to go rather than reacting to whatever good or bad fortune may come your way.

Business control is a very important concept and a measure of true success. The best advisors in our industry have reached a point where they can be extremely selective about the folks they work with...and this is a fantastic feeling. It allows them to focus on their greatest strengths instead of trying to be all things to all people. A strong referral process let's you get to that point sooner in your career.

## Referrals are a business accelerator

Leverage is a wonderful ally in growing a business. Referrals expand your reach and enable you to accelerate your growth by having other people help you get the word out. Imagine an army of hundreds, even thousands of happy clients out there telling your story to everyone they meet!

Yeah...right. Now step back and grab some reality.

Imagine instead a small group of truly excellent clients sharing your name carefully, judiciously, with one or two equally excellent friends and colleagues each year. That's more realistic and what you want anyway.

We all feel the pressure to grow our business. If you're a top producer at a wire/regional, or an independent advisor with your own shingle, you know the massive competition for HNW clients coming from every corner and the immense pressure to stay on top. Also, you may now have an entire *team* of folks looking to you for a paycheck! That's a lot more responsibility than just your own skin...so *growth* is your only option.

If you're a rookie at a major financial services firm today, you have three years to do something impressive or basically you're out. Maybe you can get picked up by a team of good producers but if you haven't had some measurable success before you hook up, you run the risk of always being thought of as the water boy by your "partners."

Worst of all is the middle-of-the-pack producer. As we speak, many companies are looking to cut the bottom quintiles of reps no matter what their length of service (LOS). Pruning the "dead wood" is a normal ritual we perform every few years and we're due. Your accounts start to look a lot more attractive in the hands of another rep who might be able to actually help those people.

Am I telling you anything you don't know? This business is built on power, strength and success. It's not a place for the sick, weak and indigent. Get tough or get out.

## *HNW clients like them*

The final and maybe simplest reason that you want to make referrals a major part of your business strategy is because top clients like them better than other marketing modalities.

My firm did a series of focus groups with million-dollar clients. In these sessions we asked a bunch of questions, including, *"How did you find your current advisor?"*

We expected to hear a cross-section of marketing approaches like seminars, cold-calls and networking, but what we heard surprised us. Everyone said *"referrals"!* Not just *most* of the people...everyone!

Now statistically, that's an aberration. You never get 100% of anything in a focus group. There's always one person who will say something different from the group if just to look odd or be obnoxious. But this question drew a uniform response.

Then it dawned on us what was going on here. HNW clients cannot even admit that there's another entrée into their world except through a referral from a trusted friend or colleague. They would never say,

> *"Oh I answered the phone at dinnertime one night and it was this charming young woman calling to manage my money...so I gave it to her!"*

Even if it were true, they couldn't say it or they risk looking dumb! So from their perspective, referrals are pretty important as well. Amazing how that works. What they want, ultimately, is for us to make referring easy, comfortable, professional, enjoyable and safe for them. Once that's done...they are much more willing to embrace the entire concept.

## *So how do you get referrals?*

There are only two ways to get referrals

**1. You ask for them.**

> *"Hey Bob how about giving me some referrals?"*

or

**2. A client offers you one.**

> *"Jim, call my friend George. He needs some help. Here's his number. Tell him I said to call."*

That's pretty much a model for anything you want in life. Naturally, there is a wide range of specific strategies and tactics within each broad category, but the prime modalities are essentially active (ask) and passive (be offered).

Networking begins as a form of the offered referral where you insert yourself into various circles of HNW folks with whom you would like to do business. You mix and mingle and look for a way to turn these social contacts into clients. If you transition too overtly into asking mode you run the risk of crashing the network.

Asking also comes in the form of sending out referral letters with the age-old phrase, *"Please list below the names of five people you feel might benefit from our services."*

Putting *"If you like us...please don't keep us a secret"* on your e-mail signature block is another form of asking.

Holding a nice dinner for clients is an offer situation, but then asking them to bring friends to the dinner is asking.

In fact, everything you could do in the entire world of referrals boils down to one of these two strategies. Is one better than the other? Can you truly expect to be offered referrals in sufficient quantity and of the quality needed to make a difference in your business and in the lives of the people you care most about?

The answer surprisingly is YES! Being offered referrals is a wonderful thing. Some call these "bird-dog" or "raving fan" referrals. You have a loyal client who has bonded to you. They refer friends and colleagues on a regular basis. They have become true disciples, advocates or champions for you in their world.

These people are fantastic and you should take great care of them if you have any. A client like this would jump right to the top of my list of special services and treatment. There is almost nothing I wouldn't do for such a raving fan.

But waiting and hoping that people generously give you referrals just doesn't work well enough to build your business on. It's not a strategy...it's wishful thinking and that's not how successful professionals work. I believe that you must learn to proactively ask for referrals if you want to be successful.

Referrals are vital to a thriving business. This all makes sense...so why aren't we asking for them? We said earlier that 75% of financial advisors never ask for referrals and 80% said the inability to ask for referrals is the biggest gap in their business. Why is that? What are we feeling when we think about referrals?

The answer is **FEAR!** And it's totally justified!

## The exploding M-16

In the early days of the Vietnam War, American GIs were issued the new "black rifle," the M-16. This was supposed to be a fantastic weapon, lightweight, durable, with a high rate of fire and great accuracy. One problem though...it got dirty instantly and then jammed, exploding in their faces, killing or badly wounding hundreds of soldiers!

So now you have soldiers who refuse to shoot their weapon...Is there something wrong with them?

## *No!*

I believe that the fact that we are NOT more proactive asking for referrals is a sign that we are completely healthy, intelligent, insightful, and caring professionals.

The referral "weapons" we've been handed (that collection of old-school referral techniques) are like backfiring guns. Not only do they miss the HNW target, but they blast hot relationship shrapnel up your nostrils. Fear and a mutinous refusal to shoot are the only sane reactions to this condition!

We're scared to death of the client's reaction and that fear is preventing many of us from taking a more active role in the process we've called "critical" to our professional success. There are four main fears we experience when it comes to referrals and we must learn to overcome them if we expect to increase our referrals:

- Fear of rejection
- Fear of risking the client relationship
- Fear of looking pushy
- Fear of looking needy

Each one of these fears links back to our totally understandable desire to be liked and respected by the client. It makes perfect human sense.

The referral techniques we have been taught (and that I am going through great pains to deprogram you of) are only viable when we don't care about the client's acceptance or have a relationship so strong that it can withstand the interpersonal shock of a clumsy technique.

So the questions become:

*How can you ask for referrals in a way that makes you feel successful, strong and confident and appear as such in the eyes of your client?*

Successful, strong and confident are three critical adjectives. They are what you want the client to feel about you and what you want to feel about yourself.

*How can you ask for referrals in a way that actually makes the client glad you asked and happy to give you great referrals?*

Oh yes...this can be done.

*Chapter 3*

# A Quick View from 30,000 Feet

In case you missed it...the entire financial services industry has been going through a period of massive upheaval. Driven by shifting client demands, an aging investor base, hyperactive regulators, schizophrenic markets, competitive pressures, and shrinking margins, our business is basically struggling to emerge into adolescence.

This change has impacted everything we do on a daily basis. Just think about some of the products and services you now offer clients as "wealth managers" that you never even *thought* of before. Programs like bridge loans, mortgages, concentrated stock collars, active indexing, and hedging strategies once were available only to a small group of elite practitioners and clients. Now everyone can do them.

These changes also have impacted our marketing strategies, making some obsolete and other more valuable. Referrals are now more important than ever before. But the training in our industry has not kept pace with this shift and we are lagging badly in the skills department as we struggle to make the move...

## From sales to service

The biggest shift in our business is not about investment products. It is about our own definition of what we do for people. We have begun the transition from a sales business to a service profession.

Granted we are not totally there yet, but the days of pitching products are almost over. The most advanced advisors in our world have become trusted partners who sit on the same side of the table as the client. We have learned to apply professional skills like comprehensive financial planning, asset allocation, absolute return strategies, and portfolio re-balancing. We actually *listen* to and care about people today and we customize our services for each client.

Our compensation models are directly aligned with clients' success and we are no longer the "broker" who profits from simply buying and selling stocks and bonds. The scope and speed of this change has been impressive. As a manager, I remember going to my brokers and actually telling them to increase the turnover rate on the assets they managed!

> *"Dave you have $60 million in assets under management, which is great...but you're only running at 1.2% annual turnover. Let's see if we can speed that up a bit...OK? How about you get out of that dog Microsoft and get into that new Dino DeLaurentis limited partnership we're offering. They're launching the new King Kong movie...it's going to be a major homerun!"*

Can you even *imagine* having a conversation like that with your manager today? I doubt it!

There are still pockets of resistance — advisors who long for the days of "touchdown bonds" and burying two points in an OTC trade. In truth, many firms seem to send confusing messages to their own advisors. They want you to be "wealth managers" but they bounce around from month to month with every new closed-end bond fund IPO.

No one said we were perfect...just radically improved. The need for revenue growth will always persist, but it can be achieved only by doing the right thing for the client. Increasingly that means a planning-based, fee-based, and trust-based relationship. Virtually everyone is in agreement on this major point.

We are maturing into one of the greatest helper professions in the world. Armed with the right skills, tools and attitudes we are ready, willing and able to serve the millions of clients desperate for our guidance. Just in time too, because we have entered...

## The Platinum Era of financial services

The term Platinum Era implies that we've already seen the Golden Era. We have. That was 1982–2000. It was an amazing time to be in this profession. My guess is you had a lot of fun during that amazing period.

Some people tell you the party is over...and they're right. THAT party *is* over, but the real party...the bigger, better party is just beginning and you couldn't have picked a more exciting time to be in this business than right now!

The Golden Era party was about performance. The Dow did a 14-fold increase from 1982 to 2000. That's not likely to happen again. More likely is a normal return that will take the Dow to 100,000 by 2025. That's great, but it's not the best part of the story.

The Platinum Era story is about the tidal wave of investors and assets that we will be handling in the next few years. The amount of money coming our way is roughly 30 times what we managed during the Golden Era!

Go back to 1982...there were no IRAs, they had just started. There were no 401(k)s...new as well. There were no rollovers. There were no Baby Boomers panic-stricken about retirement and at the peak earning phase of their careers. Oh, there were Boomers, but they weren't even *thinking* about retirement. There was no Generation X to back them up as investors (who, by the way, save the largest percentage of disposable income of any American generation).

The bottom line is all the money in all the brokerage accounts back in 1982 had less in total assets than Vanguard manages today. Investing was a hobby for a small handful of wealthy folks. Today it's a critical mission for 150 million Americans.

You might think all of this means you just have to sit there and your business will take off. Well that's the other part of the Platinum Era story...

## Everyone sees it

This future of the financial services industry is not ambiguous. It's clearly visible to anyone who wants to look. It's also seen by foreign companies. Why do you think so many European companies have been buying U.S.-based brokerage firms, insurers and money managers? Did they suddenly wake up stupid after 300 years...or do they see something exciting happening too?

Folks, the competition is growing and they are striving mightily to kick your butt! Investors today have many different places and people to go to for advice and implementation of a financial strategy — wirehouses, regionals, banks, insurance companies, CPAs, attorneys, certified financial planners, registered investment advisors, no-load mutual fund families, *Money* magazine, the Internet, CNBC. They are all flooding the investor with massive confusion and lots of choices. Somewhere in this maelstrom of money you must carve out your own niche. So even though the overall industry will thrive, your personal success is not certain by any means.

You must compete and win this asset-gathering battle. You must reach out to new HNW clients and build great relationships faster than you think. You must get really good at marketing and that takes us back to what might be the best marketing tool you have for HNW clients...referrals.

## *Growth is tough*

Even though this big picture is very bright, the process of building a successful financial practice has never been harder than it is today. Down here in the trenches the battle rages on in hand-to-hand combat. And we are running out of allies.

The market isn't helping us. It's been stuck in a trading range for five years somewhere between 9,800 to 10,800 in some time loop of endless impotence.

The media isn't helping. To keep people watching, they are forced to hype short-term thinking and intra-hour market moves. If that wasn't bad enough, we are now blessed with insights from folks like Suzie Orman and Jim Cramer! Wouldn't you love to see *their* offspring?  I never thought I'd miss Louis Rukeyser...but I do.

The government isn't helping. Between the Fed's bubble pricing strategies, Congress fighting to increase taxes, our rising trade deficit, and the seemingly blind faith in the kindness of stranger nations buying our bonds, government fiscal policy isn't engendering tremendous confidence. Not to mention the threat of terrorism, which has not abated.

Throw in the industry regulators just for fun and you have a truly challenging environment for the individual practitioner.

## *Limited window of opportunity*

Years ago, a financial advisor had an entire career to build a business. Today, you basically have five years. This shortening of the business growth curve is another one of the major changes that has taken place in our industry.

Since the Financial Modernization Bill took effect in 2000, the legislative barriers between banks, brokerage firms, and insurance companies have come down. For the first time, high-net-worth clients can have what they've always wanted — a simplified relationship with a single trusted advisor who can solve all their financial needs. Mortgages, business lending, investments, estate planning, education funding, tax minimization, all the services a client needs will be available through you. One-stop-shopping for total wealth management is here!

There are some powerful statistics in our industry on "cross-selling." They illustrate a direct correlation between the number of different "products" or "services" the client owns and client retention. The magic number is three. If you get the client into three distinct types of services (i.e., a banking, investment and insurance relationship), you have a 90% chance of keeping that client for more than five years.

One advisor (actually one team) will rise to the top as the premier player in the client's world. They will gather the vast bulk of the assets and gain control over other aspects of the client's financial (and beyond) life. If you are that advisor…you're in great shape. But if you're not, you will find it very difficult to get that client away from their premier advisor.

At a company level, brokerage firms will actually plateau in terms of assets raised organically and they will look to grow by recruiting advisors from other firms. You're actually starting to see this today with advisors opening very few net new client relationships each year and major wirehouses acquiring smaller regionals for the assets and client base.

## I know I have to grow...but how?

The mass marketing techniques of the past two decades are far less effective than they've ever been.

Cold calling is dead...somebody nail that coffin shut please before it tries to crawl out again.

Seminars and event marketing are my personal favorite business-building strategies, but they're hard to do well. I've been teaching advanced seminar techniques for years and you *can* learn to master them, but they're not for everyone. You must have a love of public speaking and a fairly healthy checkbook to make these work today.

Mass mail doesn't reach the kinds of HNW clients we want and you get nasty looks from your manager when you even *think* about doing a mailer at $0.37 a pop...so that's out.

Networking and social prospecting can work well and are closely aligned with some of the referral ideas we're going to discuss. But they are delicate instruments. Push too hard in a social circle and BANG...you're out of the circle! Networking is also less reliable at early career stages when you may not have any viable network.

Cold walking (going around to businesses during the day and introducing yourself to the owner) has a Depression-era feel to it. Maybe in rural America it still can work, but people are so security conscious today that you'd probably get arrested anyway...so it's not on my list.

Niche marketing and industry target marketing are powerful techniques, but most advisors don't understand them well enough yet to make them mainstream marketing approaches.

## This leaves you with referrals

In our modern industry with all its new rules and sophisticated investors, referrals are a fantastic way to reach out to high-net-worth clients. They have always been one of the most powerful weapons in your arsenal, but they are even more important going forward and you need to get a lot better at them.

That journey starts within the mind of the client.

*Chapter 4*

# Top Client Attributes And Attitudes

High-net-worth clients are not a mystery. After all, we are in the people business and HNW clients are the primary target for the services we offer. You would think that we might want to know a lot about them…and we do.

These characteristics and attitudes have a major impact on referrals. They combine in various ways to drive different aspects of the new referral process. They form the underlying structure and rationale for my referral strategies. Keep all of these in mind as we get into the referral strategies because they will resurface repeatedly. Also this is designed as an overview. We will be expanding on these as we move into the strategies. I just want to set the base of understanding first.

So what do we know about high-net-worth clients?

## 1. They know other people with money and have influence with them.

This is the core reality and main reason we are pursuing them for referrals in the first place. HNW clients can dramatically enhance your business if they open up their world to you in a meaningful way. Also, the folks they know are the ones who *really need your help!* You have the expertise and programs to make a difference in *their* lives and that "helping" concept is the primary driver of your referral process.

From a business perspective, however, imagine your top clients hand-carrying you around to meet all their friends and colleagues while giving you an enthusiastic endorsement with each of them. That could raise you several million in net new assets — maybe several HUNDRED million! The client may be only the visible outcropping of a giant money vein. Dig into it and you will begin to change your entire business and their lives for the better.

HNW clients move in various-sized circles we want to penetrate. Their friends and colleagues are both the right demographic and the right *psychographic*, meaning they think similarly and have similar values. For example, this is a group that generally likes using professional advisors and is willing to pay for the service and convenience. I am generalizing, of course, but these are valid assumptions.

I say "various-sized circles" because it doesn't matter how big their network is. Not all HNW clients are social butterflies who touch hundreds of other people. Many are very private folks. In this kind of networking, size doesn't matter. What's important is that your best clients are often highly powerful within whatever networks they do have. When a successful business-owner client tells their friend to take your call…the friend takes your call…with interest! That's called *influence* or *prestige* and it can make all the difference in the world of HNW referrals.

## 2. They are hard to reach.

You can't rely on simple luck to get into the world of the HNW client. It takes hard work, careful planning, and a detailed understanding of who they are and how they think.

On the other hand…this is a wealthy country. You could probably walk out your door this morning and run across more than a few millionaires on the way to work. Chances are that the businesses you pass on the way to work are owned or operated by someone who has a few bucks.

Hang around this business long enough and you will inevitably stumble across a dozen wealthy clients. Also, you may have the connections, pedigree, golf handicap, or secret handshake needed to move in those circles yourself...which is a nice thing. We can all think of a few advisors who have done well on personal contacts alone.

For the rest of us…success takes effort! Finding and capturing HNW clients and their referrals requires that we develop a strategy backed up by daily activities focused on specific, measurable goals. And for the most part, it's not a numbers game...it's an intelligence game.

## 3. HNW clients want to feel special.

Everyone wants to feel special but these folks know they *deserve* to feel special. Special is the entry point into their world. You need to start at special and work up from there. At a minimum, this means a bulletproof service model with zero tolerance for administrative errors, stupid mistakes, and dropped balls. We will expand on this in a minute.

Making other people feel special is not always easy in today's industry. For one thing, you may not have as much administrative help as you did a few years ago. Also, the level of service from our competitors has gone up. Clients are getting used to 24/7 service with instant response to problems. I think we need to begin to carve out a new realm of services that cannot be duplicated or commoditized. But before you can do that, you need to know more about what they want and how they view you today.

At the HNW client level, service goes way beyond the basics. It's now found in the little things you do without being asked that go that extra mile in anticipating client needs and desires. It's proactive and customized. And it's exhibited by an attitude that exudes from your entire staff like heat and light from a glowing fire of enthusiasm and personal concern.

## 4. HNW clients like working with winners and respect business success!

Successful people like to work with other successful people. It gives them the confidence that they're getting top-quality advice. Plus they like to see a reflection of themselves when they look at you. Displaying success in the right way and professionally conveying a message of strength, skill, and prosperity to your top clients is vital to the referral process.

This is not showmanship or pretend success. It's not about the Rolex or the Mercedes. This crowd isn't into the trappings of success. If you haven't read everything by Tom Stanley, now would be a good time. He is the author of several books, including *The Millionaire Mind* and *Marketing to the Affluent*. They will all help you tremendously.

Success is an attitude. You might call it a quiet confidence. But be careful! Judging by the way many advisors behave today, we seem to have embraced the *quiet* part and not enough of the *confidence*. We may have forsaken the critical leadership role within our relationships.

HNW clients need leadership and they value it. They know their own strengths and weaknesses and they seek to hire professionals who complement their efforts and fill in their gaps. So don't be afraid to be strong...it's what they're looking for. And it's a lot more fun anyway!

Professional humility and self-deprecation can be very good traits at times (or so I've been told), but there are other times, especially with HNW clients, when you simply must be willing and able to blow your own horn. The trick is in knowing how to honk without crossing the invisible and often shifting line between confident professional and cocky braggart.

One more thing about attitude: HNW clients like to work with positive people. Your belief system needs to have a "can do" core. They don't want a cheerleader or a positive zealot who sees nothing but the good in all things. There isn't good in all things. They want a professional who can clearly see the obstacles but who can navigate around them safely and progress toward a worthy goal.

In his book *The Wealth and Poverty of Nations: Why Some Are So Rich and Some So Poor*, historian David Landes concluded:

> *In this world, the optimists have it, not because they are always right, but because they are positive. Even when they are wrong they are positive, and that is the way of achievement, correction, improvement and success. Educated, eye-open optimism pays.*

## 5. They're busy.

HNW clients are generally not thinking about you at all. They are too busy being high net worth — building a business, running a company, or growing their own practice — to be worried about you and who they're going to refer to you today.

Let me put this in numerical terms to help you understand just how low on the mental totem pole you are. **We occupy less than two basis points of brain space in the mind of our top clients.**

This is a hard fact for many advisors to accept because you spend so much time thinking about *them*. Well, that's your profession — it's your *business* to think about them. It's absolutely NOT their business to think about you. In fact, if they *are* thinking about you too much it's probably not a good thing…so be thrilled with your two beeps!

Unfortunately, you need more brain-space to get referrals…so we need to learn some simple ways to capture more real estate in their heads without being obnoxious.

## 6. They fear referrals and have a lot to lose.

We are going to get deeper into this but always remember — **for a HNW client, referrals are like writing naked call options!** In case you forgot that from the Series 7…it means a tiny upside reward coupled with unlimited downside risk!

It is this fear that prevents them from opening up their world to you in a meaningful way. Obviously we will explore some specific strategies that will make this fear go away, or at least minimize it sufficiently to enable you to manage the process.

## 7. They are ferocious about privacy.

Privacy and confidentiality are so important in the world of HNW clients that entire industries and even countries are based on this understanding.

They don't want anyone knowing anything about their finances and they fear that you would divulge any information necessary to get a new client. Go one step further. Not only don't they want friends or colleagues to know anything about *their own* finances, but they don't want anyone thinking that they are thinking about *their friend's* finances either.

I never found an easy way to say that, but you get the idea. It's a mutual code of privacy, an *"omerta"* that can make referrals very hard to get. You will hear these folks say, "I never get involved with my friends' finances." And from their perspective, you must understand and appreciate this statement.

## 8. They admire your professional expertise.

HNW clients like working with top-tier professionals in every industry that touches their lives. They love and will pay big for real or perceived quality and knowledge beyond the ordinary. In fact, many of them are frustrated because they are willing and able to pay but can't find the quality they demand. This crosses many fields from financial services to cars, food, health, vacations, schools, homes, clothing, etc.

So are you really an investment or financial "expert"? What does it mean to be an expert? How would I know that you are an expert? Can you see any benefit to developing expertise in a particular area or investment specialty?

Take this question in another direction. Are you a *client* expert? Do you have a certain niche group of people whose needs you understand and are able to service completely? Are you the "go to" advisor for any particular group and is there a benefit to being that?

To the degree you can specialize and become an expert in something, you will increase your referrals dramatically.

## 9. They don't know your story or how to tell it to others.

Every day, your best clients are in a position to refer you to a friend or colleague...yet they're not doing it! Why not? In many cases it's because they don't know you or what to say about you. They have no story to tell. Frankly (and this is the scary part), YOU have no story to tell!

I ask hundreds of advisors each year to tell me their story and I get back a lot of compliance-approved pabulum and cookie-cutter, boilerplate bull%$#@. We've lost our way in this fog and need some strategies to cut through the haze. Only then can we begin to give our clients the concepts and words to say when a referral opportunity presents itself. First, you need a clear message...then you can tell it to the client.

# 10. They like a professional, customized approach.

It always helps to remember...

**The way you ask _for_ the referral will demonstrate the importance you place _on_ the referral.**

HNW clients don't generally respond well to the super-casual, laid-back, haphazard, random referral approach: _"So Bob...who else do you know?"_ They require a more formalized structure that recognizes the tremendous power they exert on others and the risks they run when using that power on your behalf.

I recommend asking in a very professional manner with clear evidence that you take referrals very seriously. I'll show you a great way to do that.

Also, they like total customization in almost every service you provide for them. Receiving a mass-market referral letter, for example, is an anathema to a strong relationship.

The interesting and funny part about customization (and this goes beyond the issue of referrals) is that everything you do for these clients should be made to _appear_ customized whether it really is or not. You should consider "customizing" almost every facet of your business for these folks. You may not like this but that's what they want.

One problem you may face in this area is that many major financial services firms are trying to unify or homogenize the experience clients have with every advisor. Some call this "the McDonald's theory." A burger should taste the same in Boston or Bangkok. In the mind of many HNW clients this feels like a cookie-cutter approach and they don't like it.

They don't want to be treated the same as everyone else. They're special and unique. Please understand that Baby Boomers have grown up with this message from day one. It doesn't matter that they need the exact same financial advice as 82 million of their cohorts. They want to feel that everything is customized. Make this part of your business strategy if you want to work with these folks.

These are the basic truths about HNW clients.

# 10 Truths about HNW Clients

- They know other people with money and have influence with them.

- They are hard to reach.

- They want to feel special.

- They like working with winners and respect business success.

- They are busy and not thinking about you.

- They fear referrals and have a lot to lose.

- They are ferocious about privacy.

- They admire your professional expertise.

- They don't know your story or how to tell it to others.

- They like a professional, customized approach.

You may want to refer back to this chapter periodically to remind yourself why you're doing certain things. Now, with these as the backdrop...let's get into the specific strategies that will win you some referrals.

# Part 2

# The Ten Strategies

*Referral Strategy #1*

# Develop a Referral Plan

## Concept overview:

- You need a formal, written referral plan to succeed. A plan turns a good idea into a set of concrete action steps.

- Start by listing twenty top clients you want referrals from.

- Build a Referral Intelligence File (RIF) for each client to uncover links to potential prospects.

- List twenty prospects you want to be referred to.

- Build another RIF for each of them to uncover links to existing clients who can connect you.

- Uncover specific links and use the "Basic Approach."

Your plan will become the framework for all referral-generating activities in the future. Without a plan, you are shooting in the dark…so pay attention. This is not hard at all.

The basic referral plan starts with a simple question:

**Which clients do you want referrals from?**

Bad grammar and all…that's the starting point in the entire referral process.

# Step 1: Identify twenty clients you want referrals from.

Which of your clients are viable referral mining targets? Who would you like to clone? You need to define this list and literally write the names on paper.

This is the basic first step in every referral plan. We will go deeper in a minute but this is the core list you need to build. How you decide is up to you. Your wealthiest clients are not always the ones at the top of this list. Beyond assets I look for the following criteria:

– Clients who are great networkers and who have influence with lots of people.

   *Do some research to be sure you know who the networker is in your client's family. It might not be the person with whom you talk regularly. My insurance agent regularly asks me for referrals to my neighbors. He doesn't realize I am not connected to anyone. I barely know my neighbors. On the other hand, I'm pretty sure my wife is the mayor of our town. Judging by the constant stream of phone calls that come into the house, she's a well-connected individual. If this agent were smart, he could be reaching scores of top referrals through Rebecca. Yet he never speaks to her. Big mistake! No awareness = no referrals!*

– Clients in growth industries where there is likely to be strong future potential business, such as lending, stock options and possibly investment banking.

– Clients in fast-changing or consolidating industries where there is potential for early retirement rollovers, transition 401(k)s, business sales, or stock liquidations. In addition, look for clients who may interact with industries like this.

– Clients in niche industries that you might like to penetrate. We are going to get more into Industry Target Marketing, but finding a good industry or cluster can be a massive potential target for referrals. A classic example is the custom home-building industry. Not only do these folks have money themselves, but they touch scores of other industries and business-owners with money as well.

– Clients who advise other wealthy folks. This includes the obvious centers of influence like accountants or attorneys, but can also include business managers, sports agents, top insurance executives who work with institutional clients, politicians, the list goes on.

– -Clients you like personally. This may be the most important criterion because you want to build a business around great people whom you truly care about...and you can with referrals.

I've seen advisors build huge practices working with clients who shared a particular hobby or passion. One FA I know loves to hunt and shoot. He targets people (that's bad) who have that same hobby and he has built a tremendous "quality of life" business. He's always planning trips with his clients to have fun...and he usually comes back with a few new names. The bond that forms between him and his clients transcends the money and becomes a friendship.

This type of business with "friends" is made even more possible due to the advancements in managed money programs that afford you time away from the computer and in front of people. Now you are basing your recommendations on carefully balanced portfolio construction rather than transactions.

## *Twenty names only*

There may be no end to the list of potential clients you might like to clone, but this should get you started. The good news is you're only looking for twenty people.

Why only twenty? Well...if you could take the top twenty people in your book and clone them every year...would you be happy and successful? I think so. *"But if twenty is good, forty is better, right?"*

Wrong! You will see in a minute that twenty is about all you can handle. So be selective and thoughtful when picking your top twenty. You are going to be spending a lot of time with these folks and you want to be comfortable with them from the start.

# Step 2: Gather information.

Take your list of 20 clients and build a Referral Intelligence File (RIF) on each one. Start by getting a loose-leaf notebook about two inches thick. Then enlarge and print about forty copies of the image below and begin gathering data. (I will explain the forty in a minute.)

Some of you may be tempted to jazz this up and make it more complicated...maybe even record all the data on your computer. I beg you to avoid that. All you need here is some central place you can gather and record data.

Using a loose-leaf notebook allows you to add pages with articles, pictures, documents or other items you may find that help the process. Also, something powerful happens to you psychologically when you write stuff down — you transmit information from one hemisphere of your brain to the other. This puts different parts of your mind to work on solving a problem.

*In most people the left half of the brain handles words and logic; the right half is better at art, music and intuition. When you write by hand, you are sharing an experience between the two halves, the affective (emotional) right brain and the cognitive (logical) left brain. You can now tap into the strengths of each. It's one of the reasons psychiatrists urge some people to keep a written journal or when you're really angry you often feel better after writing a letter. The act of writing often helps people put thoughts and feelings into a different perspective. Try it and see for yourself.*

Add to all this the ability to see lots of data at one time and you begin to make connections to seemingly unrelated ideas and generate subconscious creativity. This can be a powerful ally to your process. It's a way to unleash the genius within you.

*The Referral Intelligence File (RIF) worksheet*

# Name of Top Client

● **Personal World**

_____
_____
_____
_____
_____

**Professional World**

_____
_____
_____
● _____

**Community**

_____
_____
_____
_____

**Potential Referrals**

_____   _____
● _____   _____
_____   _____
_____   _____

The purpose of the RIF is to look for links to prospective referrals. Who in the client's world might benefit most from your skill and advice? And who would you most likely enjoy having as a client?

You might be amazed how little you know about your top clients. Oh sure, you can get all the basics from the account page, but beyond the superficial, how much do you really know about their world and the other people in it?

Here are some things you might look for in each category.

## Under "Personal World":

Country clubs; hobbies; favorite vacation spots; people they socialize with; play tennis, golf, sail, travel, shoot, ski with; kids' or grandkids' names and schools; favorite restaurants or types of food and wine; who built their home; contractors they use; car they drive; boat they own; plane they fly; etc.

## Under "Professional World":

Names of colleagues; competitors; suppliers; clients; board memberships; certifications they have; trade pubs they read; articles they've published; business books they write and read; meetings and conferences they attend; organizations they are in; etc.

## Under "Community":

Causes they support with time or money; clubs and civic organizations they join, charity events they host or attend; public activities they enjoy; groups they would *like* to participate in; etc.

The list goes on, but I think you get the idea. I'm looking for links to the most important people in my client's life — the folks he/she cares about most deeply. These will ultimately become the people to whom I am willing to open up my practice.

## *Do your homework*

The reason you are building this intelligence file is because top clients are way too busy to randomly think of people to refer to you. The generic question, *"Who else do you know that might be interested in our services?"* followed by the list of memory joggers is way too haphazard for these clients. It demonstrates no effort on your part and tells them that referrals are nothing more than an afterthought for you...an *"oh by the way"* sales tactic.

Instead, you want to focus them immediately on a specific person. By targeting specific people in their world to whom you *know* they are connected, you channel their energies and demonstrate care, professionalism, and preparation...all good things!

This approach is powerful, it works...AND it makes you look serious and much more successful. You're not just taking any client that can fog a mirror. You are selective about the people with whom you do business and you take the time to know who they are before asking for a referral. That elevates your entire referral process a few notches in the client's mind.

## Don't go through the trash!

Some of you might fear that this approach feels too much like the movie *Wall Street* where Bud Fox shadowed Sir Larry around town on a motorcycle and rifled through the files in the attorney's office disguised as a janitor. I am not suggesting you get a pair of night vision goggles, a 600 mm Nikon lens, and stalk your clients from the shadows.

I am talking about publicly available information that five minutes of research can begin to uncover for you. There are four places to start:

**Google** — The Internet in general is the ideal source for tons of data on anyone you might have on the list. I would Google everyone in my RIF and then start digging deeper from there. Try www.infospace.com and do a reverse lookup to get the names of your client's neighbors.

You may have clients who sit on boards of foundations or who might be members of groups that have a foundation associated with it. If so, you can subscribe to www.fdncenter.org and get the names of every board member along with other valuable information about that foundation. Foundations and endowments are a tremendous source of potential business for you and a great way to use your talents to give back to the community or a cause you care deeply about.

**The local paper** — Obviously this is a good source for social information and some company intelligence. If you have clients living in other cities, I would get the local newspaper for them. Many newspapers are available online as well. How impressive would it be for you to chat about an event that took place 2,000 miles away from you, but in which the client was somehow involved? You are clearly not the typical advisor at that point.

**The local business journal** — This drills deeper into the client's professional world and addresses business-specific issues. It's a great source of marketing information in general. Every major city has one of these and the same rule about out-of-town clients applies here too.

**The client's industry pubs** — This is an extremely powerful source of prime information on your client's core universe. There may be several publications that cover them just as we have *Registered Rep, Research, On Wall Street, Financial Planning,* etc. Find out what they read and get those yourself. You will be amazed at what you find in there. This is also a cornerstone principle for Industry Target Marketing that we will touch on in a while.

**Hobby publications** — Your top clients all have hobbies of some kind. Chances are very good that they socialize with people who have those same hobbies. Find out what they are and learn about them. You may not find names of specific referrals in these magazines, but when the client does eventually introduce you to their sailing buddy, you will know a bow from a stern and a sheet from a line. People do business with people they like...and who are like them!

## *Keep your eyes open*

Information is all around us. Sometimes, however, we need to be on a sharp lookout for the really valuable stuff.

> *Recently my wife and I were looking at vacation homes. We found one place that was particularly appealing and I began to take special notice of certain details and items in the house to see if I could gather some impressions about the sellers. I was looking for anything that might give me some insight into what kind of people they were and how I might approach a price negotiation with them.*
>
> *I noticed a horse magazine sitting on a coffee table and casually picked it up. In the subscription box was a woman's name. I made a quick mental note. Back at the hotel I hit the web and started digging.*

*Sure enough there she was! The wife had won an equestrian title only a few weeks earlier...so I guessed they had money. Horses are often seen hanging around people with money...they like getting fed. I also noticed the majority of events she had entered were in another state, which suggested their motivation to move might be strong.*

*Then I started digging up the husband and found a mother lode of data. He was a former venture capitalist and had run a few companies. There were dozens of references and connections. I was stunned by how much information I could uncover in just a half hour.*

*The point of this story is that in every article were the names of other people closely associated with this couple, groups they belonged to, charities they supported and events they attended. If I had been looking for potential referrals, I would have uncovered about twenty highly qualified prospects in under thirty minutes. And these folks were total strangers! Imagine what you could learn if you had some idea where to start digging.*

## When do I have time to do all this?

As our business has evolved, we have finally begun to realize that our job is no longer to manage the money...but to work with the people. All that wasted time and energy you used to spend picking stocks, worrying about earnings reports, designing portfolios, and laddering bonds can and should now be farmed out to full-time experts who do it much better than you ever could.

There are many paths in the financial services industry. You chose the profession that deals mainly with people...not money. The technology of money and investing is *part* of our business and you do need to *understand* it — but you need to understand people a thousand times better.

So if you're busy hunting for the next hot small-cap growth stock, studying the *alpha* and *Sortino ratio* of your portfolio, or sitting in front of your computer screen trying to will tiny numbers to move from red to green...then go be an analyst! Otherwise do what you're paid to do (which is the infinitely more difficult job by the way) — build great relationships with human beings who need your help. I'm thinking that should free up some time for you.

# Step 3: Identify twenty top prospects you would like to be referred to.

This is where the fun begins! Referrals are actually a two-way street. You start by gathering data on twenty top clients and searching for links to prospects. Now you're going to repeat the process with twenty top *prospects* and search for links to existing *clients*.

*One night early in my career as a stockbroker, I was working late in the office when the top producer in my branch came over to my cubicle and started chatting with me. I was excited. This guy never came out of his office and absolutely never spoke to one of us untouchables in the bullpen...so I was also curious.*

*He said he'd seen me working late and mentioned that hard work was one of the keys to success. I felt proud. Then he asked to see my "Hit List." I wasn't sure what he was talking about and made some dumb comment about not asking a Sicilian to see the "hit list." He was not amused and I sensed he was trying to teach me something so I decided to shut up and listen.*

*He took me into his office and pulled out a dog-eared yellow legal pad that looked like it was filled with information on every page. He tossed it across the desk to me and said, "That's my Hit List."*

*I looked in amazement at some of the names on the list — the biggest names in town — people who were on everyone's prospect database and many names that were too big to even approach. I was in awe. "You work with these people?" I asked.*

*"No you idiot...I don't work with any of them and they don't know me from a hole in the wall...yet. But they will."*

*He proceeded to explain his approach and as he did a revelation began to dawn on my rookie brain working it's way into an epiphany moment.*

*He started each year by building a list of people he wanted to do business with. Top prospects in the community that he really wanted as clients. He built the "Hit List" of these names and set to work developing links to these people throughout the course of the entire year. It was a "reverse referral list" of sorts. Who do you want a referral TO?*

*On the top of each page was a name in bold letters. Underneath the name, filling the pages in many cases was information about that person, his company, his family, clients who might know him, taped articles he had cut out of the Sun about those people, pictures, names of schools and charities...a potpourri of data, trivia, phone numbers, and tidbits of intelligence that he used to build a customized attack plan for each person.*

*It was an amazing amount of information and as he explained his process, my head started to hurt. I felt like the ape in* 2001: A Space Odyssey *as he touched the monolith for the first time.*

*Do you mean that prospecting isn't a random cold-calling game with names from the phonebook?*

*Are you saying that I can take total control of my business by deciding in advance who I want to work with?*

*It was a lot to process and he saw that I was confused, so he said simply, "Go build a list of people you want to do business with over the next year. Come back to me next week and I will get you started."*

*I came up with fourteen quality names and went to see him three days later. We sat down again and went through the list and he gave me ideas on each person about how to approach them: clubs they were members of, other clients in the office who might know them, people to stay away from because they were idiots. He really was helpful.*

*By the end of that year I was doing business with eleven out of the fourteen and one extra I added to the list later. They were not clients in today's sense of the word. I cannot say that we had a great relationship, but they bought some muni bonds or some Baltimore Gas & Electric preferreds and a few had some mutual funds. I could call them and they would take my call. Back then, that was a victory and I was thrilled.*

*How many would I have worked with if I didn't create the list?*
*Probably none! So this was a fantastic exercise and one that I*
*practice to this day.*

# Step 4: Build the RIF for prospects.

Now it's time to build List Number Two.

Find twenty people in your community that you would like to be doing business with one year from today. If you've been in the business for over an hour or two you probably have a pretty good idea of whom to target. But again, keep your eyes open. There is money all around you and hundreds of people who need your help.

The goal of this RIF is to uncover links to clients or other people already in your world who might be in a position to refer you. You're likely to be amazed at how well connected you already are to the prospects on your Hit List. If you have been in the business or the community for any length of time, you may be no more than two or three steps away from anyone you have on that list.

Start with simple items like the prospect's home address. Then search for your clients, friends, relatives and acquaintances who live anywhere near that prospect. You're trying to form a bridge from the world you know to the world you don't — from the familiar to the strange. That bridge may have a few spans...but you *can* get there. Everyone with serious money in your community is connected...believe it! It's your job to uncover those connections. Some folks call this "networking." It's just another name for the same concept: reaching new people to help.

## *The "Basic Approach"*

After you have started gathering data in your two Referral Intelligence Files (one for clients and one for prospects), you will begin to uncover potential links. Now it's time to apply the "Basic Approach." This is a very simple and comfortable technique you can employ almost anytime. It goes like this:

**– Advisor**

*"Hey Bob...it's Jim from First Hungarian."*\*

*Jim's former imaginary firm, Blowhard & Boggle, was recently acquired by a European bank.

### – Client

*"Hi Jim...how are you?"*

### – Advisor

*"Great Bob...listen I had something I wanted to chat with you about and I thought if you had a minute this might be a good time."*

### – Client

*"Sure...go ahead."*

### – Advisor

*"I have had a name of a prospective client sitting on my desk for about two months now and I was finally planning to call this guy this week, but it dawned on me that you might know him. Barbara said you guys buy computers from ACME and apparently he owns the company. I wanted to get your thoughts before I called him. Do you know Tom Stevens?"*

### – Client

*"Sure I know Tom. We've been buying from ACME for years."*

### – Advisor

*"Is he a good guy...what do you think of him generally? Do you feel he would be a good person to work with?"*

This is where the conversation could go in several directions.

*1. "Tom is a great guy. I've known him for years. He's really built that business into something nice. I think you'll like him a lot."*

*2. "Not really, I haven't had too much contact with Tom."*

*3. "That guy is a jerk. He ripped us off for defective machines last year and we are still in court over this. What a nightmare."*

OK...stop here for a second.

First...what did you just do? You are on your way to asking for a referral but first...you're probing the road ahead. How did you get Tom Steven's name? Well, you did your homework. On your last visit to Bob's office, you noticed an ACME Computer Company sticker on the back of several desktops and their printers. You asked his secretary Barbara about it and she said they buy all their computers from ACME. BINGO! You then did some research on ACME and got Tom's name.

Has it been sitting on your desk for two months? Who knows? If not, say, "two weeks." Tell the truth. You're just trying to take the pressure off the client by not tying Tom's name to him. But you could even say, *"I saw an ACME Computer sticker on your desktops and thought you might know Tom."* The point is that you uncovered a link, and now you're testing to see if it's a valid potential referral.

Notice what you did NOT say:

You did not ask for Bob's permission to call Tom. You said you were planning to call him. And you did not jump right out and ask for the referral. The subliminal message you're trying to send here is that you are very selective about the people with whom you do business. You might not want Tom Stevens at all if he's a jerk. Now, in truth, you would probably take him even if he were exporting weapons of mass destruction...but the impression you're trying to give Bob is that if *he* doesn't like Tom...neither would you.

So you're asking first, getting some feedback, and then, depending on what you hear, you're going to move into the referral part of the conversation. If Bob says that Tom is a great guy or has any positive feedback and awareness of Tom, you might say...

*"Thanks Bob, that's nice to hear. He sounds like a good guy. Do you think there is any way you could engineer an introduction to Tom?"*

"Engineer an introduction"

"Set up a lunch meeting"

"Put the two of us together"

"Get me on his radar screen"

You want the client to imagine the physical act of introducing the two of you...because that's the best-case scenario. It's a little Neuro-Linguistic Programming (NLP) technique similar to a golfer visualizing the perfect shot before hitting the ball.

On the flip side, if you hear something negative...

> *"Thanks Bob...I appreciate the insight. I am going to have to think about this. He might not be the kind of client we want at First Hungarian."*

Hey maybe that's true. If one of your top clients tells you someone is a jerk, you're definitely going to think twice before approaching the client. And in fact, you weren't planning to call Tom anyway without some kind of link to Bob, because that would be a cold call and ineffective at best.

At this point, depending on the tone of the conversation with your client, you might push a little further. Bob might be reacting too quickly and given a second chance to amend his comments, might come up with something better to say about Tom. Or else you might be able to get some information of value.

You also might turn your specific probe into a broader referral conversation. If the Tom thing doesn't work, you might say something like this:

> *"Bob, the reason I asked you about Tom is because of our specialty in business lending. We are in a unique position to help companies grow with funding at interest rates well below Libor. If you know anyone who runs a business of any kind...this might be extremely helpful to them."*

This "Basic Approach" works in most cases and is simple, effective, and professional. When you combine it with some of the other things we're going to cover, it becomes even more powerful.

Remember, referrals are a process, not a momentary snapshot conversation. Everything ties together to create a total referral approach...so this is only the first step.

The most important parts here are the fact that you did your homework and went to the client with a specific name. You leave the client with the impression that you are a much more thorough professional and that you take referrals very seriously.

You also leave them feeling like they have a certain amount of "ownership" of your business — a personal stake in you. Not a responsibility to help you grow, but an ability and a power to share your extraordinary services and expertise with friends and colleagues. You give them that power and you encourage them to use it wisely under your guidance.

*Referral Strategy #2*

# Provide Excellent Service

## Concept overview:

- Great service is mandatory for top clients. They expect it and your competition is giving it to them.

- Conduct a thorough self-assessment of your service model followed up by an assessment from your top clients.

- Manage client expectations using the "tough love" approach to better control your business.

- Learn to anticipate the needs of top clients and deliver extraordinary service beyond their expectations.

- Build a great partnership with your assistant!

In today's hyper-competitive industry, what defines top-quality service? In simplest terms it is expectation minus reality. The client expects something and you deliver less...poor service. Deliver more...great service.

I go into Nordstrom every few months to buy ties, socks and miscellaneous items. Every time I go they remember my name, size, color preference and styles. I have no idea how they do this. Maybe they have Las Vegas-style hidden security cameras with face recognition software and a computer database of all their shoppers' preferences and past purchases. This would be linked up to a communication system that beams the information directly to the department you're walking toward...and someone on the floor is alerted to your presence. It wouldn't surprise me. However they do it, I love it and it's very impressive service.

Another favorite example is the Four Seasons Hotel. Whatever time I arrive, the room is always ready with a basket of fresh fruit and iced waters with a nice little note from the manager welcoming me back. Even after getting in at 3:00 in the morning from a delayed flight...the fruit and the ice are both fresh.

They also remember your name thanks to a simple electronic touch. The valet is connected to the lobby staff with one of those Secret Service ear microphones. When you drive up he asks your name and it's picked up by the doorman and the desk clerks. By the time you reach the front desk, they have your reservation pulled and the key waiting — a nice touch and a very warm welcome!

This is wonderful stuff and it keeps me coming back, but all excellent service providers run a risk. What happens if I walk into Nordstrom and they don't remember me or someone doesn't walk over immediately to lend a hand? Or if the hotel room isn't ready and there's no fruit or note. My expectations have been set at a very high level and I would probably be disappointed.

In this way, providing great service is a combination of actually delivering the service and setting reasonable expectations for what you, as a business person, can and are willing to deliver. In both cases, these companies seem to have made a major commitment to excellence and have never failed to meet this standard in my experience. Can the same be said about you?

You have to make a core business decision here. How much are you willing and able to do for your top clients? Can you do this for everyone? I would say not, so you need to begin to distinguish the service you provide to those very best clients. For your top people, you need to set the bar high and continually raise it a bit over time. These folks expect the best and are being pursued by firms who understand this. In the world of private banking, the word "no" is rarely heard. The entire attitude is one of "let's find a way to make anything work!" That should be your guiding philosophy.

## *Service & referrals*

Service and referrals go hand –in hand. The client uses a simple equation in their head as they relate service and referrals:

### The way you treat me is how you will treat my referral!

Make me happy…you've got a great chance of getting referrals. Not a guarantee, but the odds are good.

Make me unhappy and you're pretty much down to zero probability of referrals. In simplest terms...if it takes you three hours to call me back...you're screwed. Don't bother asking me for referrals. If you keep messing up my paperwork, losing documents, mishandling minor administrative issues...you are depleting the good-will account and decreasing your chances of ever getting any friends from me.

The world of client service is complex and multi-faceted. Often, many of the typical service-type issues are beyond your direct control. You must rely on your firm, for example, to develop readable statements and timely administrative procedures that solve client problems.

## *The Rule of 100*

Just to put this service discussion in some perspective…it helps to remember that a happy client is the potential source of 100 referrals over the course of your relationship.

Whenever I'm talking to or interacting with a client in any way, I always try to visualize that client standing in the doorway of a large ballroom filled with their friends, colleagues, associates, neighbors and relatives. Right after our interaction, they will go back into that ballroom and talk to the people in their world. This image encourages me to make each interaction a positive experience for the client. I want them in the best possible frame of mind when they touch the most important people in their world.

Does this put a lot of pressure on those moments? Sure it does. But our entire business is about interacting with clients and making them feel great in the process. Each one of those moments is your "game time" and they call for you to be at your best. Chimpanzees with darts can pick stocks. Fourth graders with laptops can allocate portfolios. Managing people is your job! If you want to generate tremendous referrals from your top clients, I think you need to keep this reality in mind.

You never know when and where a client will have a chance to refer you to someone. You might be talking to them this afternoon and they might be on their way to the annual partner's meeting in Boca this afternoon. How nice would it be to leave them with a positive feeling about you just before that event?

Or if you prefer the alternative scenario: imagine having an argument with that same client in the afternoon.

> *"Dammit Bob, we are trying to solve that problem but my assistant is getting the run-around from New York and we just don't have an answer. Calling five times a day isn't going to make it happen any faster!"*

I actually overheard this exact conversation in a branch office and was stunned. Now I know we all have those PITA clients, but there had to be a better way. Assuming this advisor wanted referrals from this client...what do you think the chances are at this point?

Every interaction should leave a client feeling good about you in some way. When you stop to consider the actual number of interactions you really have with your top clients in a given year, you may be surprised to realize just how few there are. It doesn't seem that way because we think about our top clients in our sleep! We figure that they're thinking about us too. Truth is they're not...so you've got to make each moment count.

## So how do you make clients happy?

Obviously, the answer is different for each client, but there are some basic issues that regularly come up in client focus groups and in conversations. Surprisingly, rate of return and investment performance are not the top considerations. Most clients are far more interested in things like:

### Responsiveness

The basic question is, "How quickly and intelligently do you respond to my needs?" To make people feel important...speed is essential. Some action taken immediately is a lot better in the client's mind than perfect action taken slowly.

So the first part is rapid response. The second part is quality of response. How carefully do you handle my concerns and problems?

Top clients realize that there are going to be administrative issues from time to time. The check was lost, the payment went to the wrong address. These things happen all the time. It's rarely the problem itself that troubles the client; it's much more the way you handle it and make it go away in a reasonable time frame that counts.

For your top twenty client list (the ones in your Referral Intelligence File), I recommend a maximum of a one-hour callback time, preferably less than that. Frankly, if this were one of my top clients, someone on my team would handle that problem right then and there...no callback needed. This is a drop everything, "Bat Phone" response.

Oh...and when I say "Bat Phone," I am talking about 24/7/365 response. I actually give my clients a special laminated business card with my cell phone number on the back. Someone on my team is reachable at any time day or night to handle critical situations. If I'm on a plane...the number rolls over to my partner or top assistant.

Now you may disagree with this...I understand. Many advisors tell me that they would never want a client calling them at 3:00 a.m. All I can ask you is, *"Who do you want them calling?"* The good news is that this would be a very rare occurrence. Top clients simply do not abuse the Bat Phone. They're smart folks who understand the value of your time or else they wouldn't be on your top twenty list in the first place.

But lest there be any doubt, I tell them when I give them the card... *"Commissioner Gordon never called Batman at 3:00 a.m. for a cat up a tree! So I trust you to use this power wisely. But if you need me...I will be there!"*

When my clients are the most worried and in need of guidance, I want my face to immediately pop into their mind. I am more than happy to lose a little sleep in order to protect their peace of mind and to ultimately grow my business with these kinds of people. Any average advisor can be responsive from 9:00 to 5:00. Only the top pros will do it the rest of the day. And in the global world of big money (where some of you may want to play), the clock has no meaning.

## Genuine concern

How much do you care about my situation and my needs? Are you listening to me or are you just taking a breath before it's your turn to talk again? What kinds of questions are you asking me and do they reflect my issues or your agenda? Are you really interested in me and my family or just my money and the fees it generates for you?

There is no way I know of to teach an advisor how to have genuine concern for clients. You either have it or you don't. Most of the advisors I've met, however, do have this level of concern but many are lacking the interpersonal communication skills needed to actually show it to the client.

We've developed a training program called **"How to Talk So Clients Will Listen & Listen So Clients Will Talk."** We call it "Talk/Listen" for short. The title was taken from a popular children's book by Adele Faber and Elaine Mazlish that you should read. It's very instructive for clients as well. Of course they had "Kids" for "Clients" in the title, but many of the same rules apply to both groups. In this training program we discuss the five basic strategies of great client communication. If you would like more information on how to participate in this program, just e-mail me at fmaselli@ixisag.com.

## Directness & honesty

How do you interact with me when things get tough or something goes wrong? Are there hidden performance or fee "surprises" that pop up in my portfolio? Do you do what you say you're going to do? Does everyone on your team?

When I say "honesty," I'm not talking about the legal, compliance meaning of that word. I assume that we are all trying our best for the client all the time. What I mean more is the nature of the bond between client and advisor. Is there openness between us or guarded caution? Are we able to have frank discussions about any concern or are we walking on eggshells around each other? Are there unspoken issues or baggage between us that get in the way or color our interactions? Is there a fear of being judged or taken advantage of that leads to cautious conversations and incomplete information?

If these things sound like relationship issues to you, you're right. This is what it means to be in a people business. It astonishes me that we claim our profession is all about "relationships" and we spend virtually no time training in the development and conduct of those relationships. Somehow we're all just expected to know how this works. We call ourselves financial advisors or consultants and we concentrate all our effort on the "financial" part while ignoring what it means to be an "advisor" or "consultant." Those are massively important words that carry huge emotional, psychological and moral baggage. I say it's time we mastered both parts of our world...the money and the people. We will help you so get in touch with me to learn more.

The biggest single thing I can suggest in the area of client treatment is to be...

## *A promise keeper*

Yes, I know there's a religious group called the Promise Keepers, but I'm talking about a religion of a different sort — the one that believes in faithfully keeping my word to clients.

Every day we make a dozen promises to clients. Some of them are tiny little promises and others are major commitments. In truth, they are all critical and we must do a better job of delivering on these promises.

Let me give you a scenario and suggest a method of handling promises that will make your life a whole lot better and dramatically increase the likelihood of getting referrals from your clients.

*LIGHTS UP*

*The scene – a typical office in any financial services firm in America. You are seated at your desk with coffee and bagel, punching keys on a computer keyboard.*

*The phone rings. You answer it.*

**– You**

*"Hello, Blowhard...I mean First Hungarian...Jim Advisor."*

**– Client**

*"Good morning Jim…it's Bob Client."*

**– You**

*"Hi Bob…how are you?"*

**– Client**

*"Great Jim…I was calling with a little problem and I needed some help."*

**– You**

*"Sure Bob, what's up?"*

**– Client**

*"I just received my monthly statement for July and I can't seem to find that check I sent in. I'm sure I sent it and it should appear somewhere on the statement but I just don't see where it hit the account. Can you help me track this down?"*

Here's your basic plain vanilla administrative problem — nothing fancy, but a measurably important issue that's likely to arise on any given day. What would you say?

**– You**

*"Of course, Bob…let me do a little research and I'll get back to you."*

**– Client**

*"Thanks Jim. I'll wait for your call."*

*(You both hang up.)*

What did you just do?

Right…you made a promise! ***"I'll get back to you."***

Now watch what happens. Einstein's Theory of Relativity kicks in. An hour goes by…two hours. Your day is heating up. The phone is ringing, clients are coming in…you have a meeting over lunch…it's a busy day.

What has happened to the size of the promise you made to old Bob? It's begun to shrink. By 3:00 that afternoon you may have totally forgotten you ever had the conversation.

Simultaneously, what has happened to the size of the promise in Bob's mind? It has GROWN!

Bob has been standing by the phone waiting for you to call. What does he know? He assumed all you needed to do was punch up a few keys on the computer and you would instantly have an answer. How difficult can that be? This is the age of computers and instant Internet gratification, isn't it?

Two days later, Bob calls back!

*"Hey Jim, any luck on that problem?"*

Your mind races...what the heck is Bob talking about? What problem?

*"Bob...refresh my memory, buddy, what was this problem?"*

*(FADE TO BLACK)*

You've just witnessed a typical scenario that occurs about a thousand times a day in service organizations all over this nation!

Are you getting any referrals from Bob? No way! In fact, if you do this a few more times you will lose Bob entirely.

So what should you do?

One alternative would be to not make the promise in the first place:

*"Sorry Bob, I can't help you find that check...I'm just too busy!"*

As much as you might want to say that, especially for a simple admin situation, that's obviously not a good idea...so I'm not suggesting that you stop making promises. Frankly, that's impossible. But we need to get into the business of **keeping** promises. This is where we turn to the other side of the service issue...managing client expectations. I told you that top clients should get top service and that's true, but you can't let service run your entire business.

*Wait...what did you say?*

I said you can't let service run your entire business.

At the end of the day...you are not *only* in a service business. You have a host of other critical jobs that comprise the totality of being a financial professional. Start that list with asset gathering. If you don't raise huge money...you won't be here. Then you have to manage that money. Hopefully you've figured out that there are thousands of people better equipped to do that than you and you're using them for the bulk of your clients, but you must keep your hand in that game to some degree. Then there's managing a team of people like your assistants or partners. You also have to deal with management and compliance issues. What about advanced skill training? The list goes on.

The bottom line is that we don't have the luxury to devote 100% of our efforts to serving clients. Yes, that's ultimately what the result of our business efforts come out to. But on a day-to-day basis, you must allocate your time and energy carefully among all these demands or you will run your ship aground.

To help you do this, I recommend a philosophical approach called...

## *TOUGH LOVE*

The cornerstone of Tough Love is LOVE! I am going to help my clients in any way I can and I know that they are my lifeblood. No one is questioning that fundamental truth. But given the realities of a demanding business, I need to inject a little toughness into the mix. Using the example from before, I would ask one more question before making my promise:

### – You

*"Bob, of course we will find that for you...just tell me one thing before I get started. How critical is this to you? Because if it's **normal priority** then I usually handle all my administrative tasks on Fridays. Is it OK to call you back on Friday with an answer to this question?"*

95% of the time the client will say,

*"Sure...Friday's fine."*

5% of the time you may hear...

*"I'm sorry Jim...I'm on my way to the accountant this afternoon and I need that information as soon as possible."*

Wouldn't that be good to know?

You accomplished several things by asking that tough love question:

First, you gave yourself permission to handle the situation on Friday, which means that you don't have to drop everything you're doing to solve a problem. This is a version of what we call "time blocking." You can now time-block Bob's problem and put it out of your mind until it needs attention.

Without some effective form of time blocking, you're running your day by crisis management. You're playing prevent defense. Whenever a client calls with a situation, you abandon whatever you are working on to handle their problem. How can you ever get any work done? How will you ever be able to do all those other things when every externally driven event derails you from your mission? You can't function effectively that way...and you know it. This is a simple strategy that allows you to combat crisis with organization and preparation.

The second thing you've done is effectively and professionally managed Bob's expectations about how you will handle his administrative problems. You've let him know in a very positive manner that you are certainly going to handle this situation and make it right...but you're not going to drop everything to do it.

In fact, if you DID drop everything, you might be sending a dangerously wrong message that does not serve your long-term relationship goals.

Managing expectations is a critical skill to develop early in your career. Once clients learn that you handle things in a consistent manner, they will buy into your approach and come to rely on your structure. The key element is fulfillment.

You promised to call back on Friday...so what do you do?

You call on Thursday! That's called "exceeding expectations" and it is essential to creating an image of superior service in the mind of a top client.

Oh, by the way…what if you don't have an answer on Thursday…what do you do then? You got it! Call anyway and say…

> *"Hey Bob…I'm calling to follow up on that statement problem we were having."*

I stress "we" because it's not the client's problem anymore. You've made it YOUR problem.

> *"I told you I'd get back to you on Friday and I know I still have a day left on my promise, but it looks like we won't have an answer by tomorrow. The case is proving to be a little more complicated than I had anticipated and I'm going to need a few more days to get this done. I will call you on Tuesday with a resolution. This has been elevated to **high priority** and my whole team is on top of it. So just hold on a bit longer."*

You are scoring major points with this client even though you didn't solve his problem. This is how clients come to rely on you as a person who gets things done and keeps his word. By the way, notice how we bumped it up from "normal" to "high" priority?

These two items help you create the proper relationship environment for getting referrals. You can just hear Bob telling a friend, *"Hey my financial guy is great. He calls me back like clockwork and always does what he says he's going to do."*

That's nice!

I spend this time on service and "promise keeping" not necessarily because service will ever get you any direct referrals. Good service will set the tone for a positive referral expectation and discussion. I truly don't think you can expect referrals from clients who think your service stinks.

## You're probably confused now

First I said you had to provide "Bat Phone," 24/7 service to your top clients. But then I told you to handle them with Tough Love and make them wait until Friday for an answer. This sounds like matter and anti-matter. How can these two realities coexist without blowing each other up?

Service is provided along a continuum ranging from an all-hands-on-deck immediate reaction — even anticipation — to a more relaxed response. You must use your professional judgment to decide when and how to apply the appropriate level and type of response to the situation. Your top twenty clients simply start at the higher end of that range. If you start them at the very top, you have no place to go but down. Plus I would argue that the energy needed to maintain that high a level would eventually cripple your business model. So managing expectations becomes a balancing act.

Early in your career you will probably lean toward the maximum service model. I used to run a daily portfolio P&L for a $250,000 client and run it down to his office every afternoon by 4:30! I never understood why the other brokers and my manager were laughing at me. This just seemed like excellent service to me.

At some point you wake up and realize a few things about clients and their demands. Then you may wish you had trained them better earlier in the relationship because it's easy to go *up* in service quality but much harder to go *down*. Dropping the P&L delivery service lost me the client, which turned out to be a very good thing for my business and the dawn of my Tough Love approach.

## *How to get them to appreciate you*

As we said, great service is just the entry point to a HNW relationship. It does not guarantee you referrals; it merely makes them possible. Now the question becomes — How do you let the client know that the service they're getting is special? How do you help them appreciate it without being too heavy-handed? And how do you turn that appreciation into a catalyst for more and better referrals?

First, you cannot crow about everything you do for a top client. Forcing them to focus on each incident in an attempt to squeeze some appreciation out of each interaction would be counterproductive at best. Try a different approach.

## *It's all small stuff*

One FA I know has a simple philosophy about client service. He told me, *"Never sweat the small stuff...and it's all small stuff."* That became the title of one of those mini-self-help books, but he was a few years ahead of them as I recall. Here's what he told me:

*My approach is to make clients feel that there are no requests I can't handle. Nothing is too big to worry about or panic over. This is a very calming and professional tone. Not that I would downplay the need or the severity of the issue, but I let them know that once it's in my hands...it's as good as done. We are on our way to a solution.*

But, I wondered; if everything is minor, then how do you generate any recognition for the exceptional service you provide? He continued,

*When necessary, I will let the client know that some of the "small stuff" is a little bigger than others. This has become a subtle signal that my team and I are burning the midnight oil to solve a client issue. All of this work is done with a smile and grace no matter what the client may need. My team works very hard and the clients have bonded to my staff as much as to me, if not more.*

He jokes with his clients about his assistants. I heard him tell one client, *"George, after this project, I'm going to have to send Maria to Hawaii for a week. So you will have to call me while she's out."* George got the message that his request was a little bigger than usual and that Maria (the assistant) was actually the promise keeper on this case (as they are on most cases)!

*My clients know how hard we work for them and they are very appreciative. If they're not...I get rid of them! If they are ever abusive or rude to my assistants...they're gone! I can always find another million dollar client. I can't find another assistant like Maria or Paula! This is also why the best support people in the branch and in New York (headquarters) bust their butts to help me get things done. Without them I would be dead in the water. I let them know how much I appreciate them all the time.*

Sounds like a winning philosophy to me. Adapt it and make it yours!

## Your assistant

Your most valuable teammate in the execution of your service model (if not all areas) is your assistant. You might have several assistants on your team, or you might share with several other producers. The number doesn't matter. What matters is how well you work together to take great care of clients. And that takes some time to discuss.

The role of the assistant is unique in our world. They wear multiple hats and are pulled in many different directions every day. The pressures on them are incredible and very few people stop to think much about this...so take a second here and let's explore their world.

Your assistant must work with multiple groups of people, each of whom has different expectations of excellence.

They interact with your firm's operations department and handle highly complex administrative tasks that would probably fry your circuitry at first glance. To solve problems, they must often cajole, beg, bribe and frequently harass other people into helping them. When things run smoothly...it's just expected. When things get fouled up, the assistant is often sitting right in the middle of the mess and must get it cleaned up even though they didn't make it. This must all be done seamlessly without involving or distracting you...the delicate genius!

Your assistant works very closely with your clients...which can be great sometimes and a nightmare at others. The assistant/client relationship is a complex and important one. Ideally you want the client to feel so comfortable with your assistant that you don't even need to *know* about administrative issues. They are handled by the expert.

But many clients don't treat the assistant the same as they treat you. Little Mary Sunshine transforms into Ilsa She Wolf of the SS when you're not on the phone. And you sit there wondering why your assistant is so frustrated with that wonderful client. They sometimes want to scream at you, *"It's all a lie...this client is Satan's spawn!"*

On the flip side...your assistant may not know just how important the client is to you and may not treat the client with the same level of care as you would. To an overworked assistant, another client problem is just more work, more fighting with headquarters, more papers to gather and file. This is a tough, tedious job where the expectations are high, the resources are low, and the demands just keep on coming.

At the top end of the difficulty scale, your assistant must deal with you! That's like eight hours a day of ABC's *Wide World of Sports* — the thrill of victory...the agony of defeat! An assistant is often forced to act like the graphite rods in the nuclear reactor — counterbalancing and controlling your emotional explosions to prevent a meltdown.

Given all this, your assistant must be an extraordinary person with several diverse skills. It really is one of the most difficult jobs in this industry and it almost never gets the recognition (or compensation) it merits from management, clients, or even advisors.

So how do you find and work with a great assistant? How do you create a partnership that builds and nurtures great relationships with the clients? I cannot go into all the details or complexities of this relationship. It could be a book by itself. So let me share a few thoughts specific to the subject of referrals that might help get you started.

## *Assistants and referrals*

Talk with your assistant about your team's referral approach and ask them what they think. You might also ask them to read this book. They are your critical allies in the referral process and should be in step with you all the way. In fact, they may have ideas you would never have thought of to improve client communication, service, and even your own business process. You begin to unleash the power of true partnership by making your assistant a core part of the entire program immediately.

Your assistant is the front-line of all client service issues. They are the ones who have to deliver on the promises you make. So first, be careful what you promise and make sure it can be delivered. Second, be certain your assistant has the resources and support they need to get problems solved.

Your assistant doesn't need or want you involved in a service issue 99.99% of the time. Rushing in to "save the day" is not a good idea and will mostly complicate the problem or screw up a relationship they've carefully nurtured. What is needed is a certain degree of empathy and appreciation for their effort — a recognition that even the most mundane tasks (to you) require skill, time, and a bit of magic to accomplish.

Treat your clients with respect. Your assistant will pick up on subtle and not-so-subtle clues from you about the client. If you slam down the phone and rip into a client after a tough conversation, your assistant may begin to reflect those attitudes consciously or subconsciously. Even worse, they will lose respect for you for behaving so badly.

If you want to create a team culture that truly cares for people, then live that philosophy every day. Respect for and love of clients is not something you turn on like a switch. It's a permanent feeling in your office and it comes through in all interactions.

Your assistant is your professional partner and you both need skills and advanced training to succeed. The firm will provide the basics but you may want to consider augmenting that effort with programs such as the Strategic Coach. They have a great workshop for teams that will help you get to a higher level. Check them out at www.strategiccoach.com. Another group called SA Training offers a newsletter and targeted training for assistants. Find them at www.SATraining.com.

A great assistant can be a tremendous benefit to your business in many ways. Building and strengthening that relationship may be one of the most important things you do for your career.

----------------------

## NOTE:

If there were one book to read on the subject of great service, it would be Harry Beckwith's *What Clients Love*. Please devour it from cover to cover! He has nailed the topic of professional client care and his insights and stories will take you to new levels of success. Plus it's tremendous fun to read!

*Referral Strategy #3*

# Position Referrals From Strength

## Concept overview:

- You are a financial professional with unique and powerful skills. Without your help and guidance, thousands of HNW investors in your community will never reach their financial goals.

- That philosophy can actually become the cornerstone of your referral approach.

- If you can adapt this approach to fit your style, you never need to look like you're struggling or desperate for business again.

- Doing this without sounding cocky or arrogant appeals tremendously to high-net-worth investors!

- If you do not believe...it will not work!

This is a major philosophical issue and it may be the most difficult part of the new approach to referrals that I am espousing. It will work very well with top clients but it will not work at all unless you make a major shift in your thinking...starting with this fact.

**Referrals are not about clients helping you grow your business.**

**They are about you being willing, on a limited basis, to help the people your clients care most about.**

The end result may still be a bigger business, but the journey toward that end makes all the difference and with this approach you will arrive in much better shape.

## Won't they see through that?

An advisor asked me, *"Frank, that's clever and all, but won't my clients see through this as just another referral pitch?"* He was totally sincere and a bit frustrated. After decades of conditioning to believe that we are mere sales people who must resort to using Jedi mind tricks, clever schemes, and catchy phrases to get people to do something against their will, he expected that this was nothing more than another of those.

If you believe this is nothing more than another ruse or the latest referral technique...then it is! The client will most assuredly see through it because there's nothing really there. A thin mist of confidence cannot obscure the underlying flaws in the age-old model. *"Give me referrals to help me grow my business"* is a deeply ingrained paradigm that will die hard and take you with it.

## Doctor You

Imagine for a minute that you are a highly skilled biochemist. You've been working for a decade on developing a vaccine for a painful and debilitating disease and now you've found it! What would you do?

You would tell the world about it and get it into the hands of as many people as possible...I'm assuming. You created it to be used, not to be hidden under a rock. If this thing really worked, you would have a moral obligation to shout the story from the rooftops and make sure people paid attention!

Now let's stretch that fantasy one step further. Imagine that there is only a very limited supply of this vaccine and it is extremely hard to make. And further imagine that nearly everyone you know has the disease...your friends, relatives and co-workers. Now what would you do with that vaccine? That may shift the "marketing strategy" a bit.

Chances are, you would climb down from the roof and go to the people you love the most and offer them first crack at the cure. You would be selective and careful about whom you told. You might even make a list of those who would be offered the vaccine and those who would not. As much as you would *want* to save everyone…you couldn't. Some would be saved and others would have to take their chances because you have a limited supply.

Now in the real medical world, they would probably offer it based on greatest need first…so this is where my analogy breaks down…but you get where I'm going with this.

In our world, the disease is Financialis Lacaplanatosis. The patient is either missing a plan entirely or has a very weak one that's almost totally nonfunctional. A huge number of people suffer from this disease and the effects are very serious. Investors by the millions are going to perish on the road to their financial goals. They don't have the slightest idea what they need to do and don't have the discipline needed to succeed.

Financially, they will probably die without you. You are the cure! Your expertise is the vaccine they need to survive and you have an obligation to share this with as many people as you can reasonably handle.

That's the first part of the philosophy. You must believe that you truly *are* the cure. There are a lot of financial advisors in your market and I strongly recommend that you begin by becoming and *believing* that you are among the very best of them.

OK…right there we lost a few followers. Many of you don't believe that you *are* among the best. In fact, you can probably name at least a dozen competitors in your town or even colleagues right in your own office who are a lot better than you.

This lack of personal and professional conviction is a major problem that will prevent you from implementing the Strength Referral philosophy. Without your belief system firmly implanted, you will have a hard time convincing clients of your value. And so a "strength referral" will seem like just another sales approach to them.

## *Redefine success*

How you define success may be part of the problem. Traditionally, we have used "gross production" to measure ourselves, but that yardstick is nothing more than our industry's way of keeping score internally. It has no positive bearing on the relationship nor any importance to the client. It might even have a negative correlation. So let's craft a better definition of "The Best Advisor," one that can include you even if the ink is still wet on your Series 7 exam. These are few of the questions I would use to define excellence in today's business:

- Do you genuinely like and care about your clients?

- Do you always put their interests ahead of your own or those of your firm?

- Do you work exceptionally hard for them?

- Do you take the time to get to know them and customize your recommendations to their individual needs?

- Are you a fantastic listener? Do you listen actively with care and interest?

- Can you hear what's not being said as well as the words?

- Are you skilled in the science of finance and can you solve the complex problems of top clients?

- Are you willing to admit you don't know everything and do you know where to go to get the answers you may need?

- Do you have a team backing you up with the right mix of services and products to accomplish the mission?

- Do you stay intellectually alert, current and on top of cutting-edge strategies?

- Are you proactive and able to anticipate client needs or simply reactive to markets and requests?

- Do you keep your promises no matter how small?

- Is your word good and your reputation solid?

- Do you genuinely appreciate your clients and let them know?

- Can you cut through the clutter and help clients understand what they're doing and why?

- Are you clear, direct and inspiring in your communication or do you confuse and depress people when you talk?

- Do you give people the confidence and conviction needed to implement a viable, long-term investment strategy?

- Do you seek a deeper, more disciplined investment process and analysis or are you a "hot dot chaser"?

- Are you a partner in your clients' total success not only with investments but in other critical aspects of their world?

- Are you linked up with other top professionals who can help your clients with a broader array of needs?

If you can answer all or even most of these questions positively, I don't care what your production numbers look like. You have a right to count yourself among the best in this business. And you have a sacred obligation to spread the word about what you're doing for people. Every person you do *not* reach is at the mercy of *Money* magazine, CNBC, their brother-in-law, or that nut Cramer (who may represent the apotheosis of media sponsored financial titillation).

## *Now...selectivity*

The reality of your business is that you cannot take on 500 new clients in any one year and still cure folks. The vaccine gets too diluted the more you spread it around ...so you have to be selective. You must go first to the people you care the most about — your top clients — and make it available to the people in their world...again on a selective basis.

I estimate that the average financial advisor can handle fifty new HNW clients every year. That averages out to one new client per week. If that seems like too big a number, you may be comparing it to the dismal new account numbers we've seen over the past several years in the industry.

Most advisors today are opening far less that five new HNW accounts per year and they think that's OK and normal. You are much better than that. Even the largest and busiest teams of advisors have the investment processes and service capacity for twenty new clients per year.

If you are so strained that you can't handle that inflow, then something is wrong with your business model and you need to take a look at it immediately. There is no status quo in this business. You are either continually growing or slowly liquidating. I'm going to assume you agree with this, so we can set twenty new relationships as our target and move on.

So who gets to work with you? Who deserves that honor, privilege, and good fortune? Isn't that a much better state of mind from which to approach referrals (if not all of life) than one of scarcity, desperation, and fear? And if you can successfully pull off this attitude shift without coming across as boastful or arrogant, can you see where this approach actually would appeal to HNW clients?

Here's how I might script a Strength Referral conversation:

## *The Strength Referral script*

The scene is a dinner meeting with Jim, the financial advisor, and Bob, his client:

### – Advisor

*"Hi Bob, it's good to see you. How have you been?"*

### – Client

*"Hi Jim. I'm great. How are you?"*

### – Advisor

*"Great Bob. I'm glad we had this chance to get together. It's been too long."*

### – Client

*"I agree. We should try to do this more often. So what's new in the investment world?"*

General conversation continues for a while with a discussion of the markets, Bob's portfolio, and other small talk until the appropriate moment, which would be roughly one half of the way into the meeting.

### – Advisor

*"Bob, there was another topic I wanted to discuss with you tonight. Actually, it's been on my mind for a while and I was waiting until I felt the time was right to bring it up."*

### – Client

*"Sounds serious...what is it?"*

### – Advisor

*"I've been noticing several trends in the investment industry today and because of them, my team and I are making a major effort to reach out to selected investors and help more people get back to reaching their goals. Investing today has become a lot more confusing. You may have noticed this yourself. There is conflicting advice coming from all the so-called experts and massive confusion from the media. This is not new, but it's gotten worse recently and I've decided to ramp up my efforts to help people overcome this confusion. Which is where you come in."*

You're setting the stage for referrals by expressing concerns about the confusion and bad advice that's out there in the marketplace. In this way, referrals become less about you growing your business and more about helping people with their goals. It positions you to discuss your team as a dedicated group of professionals who truly are different and who care about their clients...which is all true!

### – Client

*"How can I help?"*

### – Advisor

*"I told you I was waiting for the right time to discuss this. Over the last few years [months], my team and I*

*have really enjoyed having you as a client. My sense
is that you are feeling pretty good about us too. We've
put together a really solid financial plan for your family
and I think you probably have a feeling that we do
things pretty well at First Hungarian."*

A quick little relationship recap. Why are you together? What does the client like and appreciate about your services and approach to investing? Build this conversation on top of positive feelings.

*"We have decided to open our doors up to the friends,
relatives and colleagues of our top clients. It just
seems to us to be the best way to expand our reach.
Our commitment to you extends to the people in your
world that you care most about. But this is not
something we can open up to all our clients. I want to
manage our growth carefully because our entire
business is built on top-quality advice and service."*

The concept of managing your growth assures the client that they are still the number-one priority in your world. It also makes you look like an intelligent business professional. You do NOT need to say anything like, *"Giving us referrals means we will have more time to work for you since we won't have to market or make cold calls to grow."* That's the old-school "implied threat" approach and is totally unwarranted with a top client.

*"Frankly, we chose you first because we like working
with you and also because you have some people in
your world that we would be very interested in talking
with. It's possible that they would benefit tremendously
from the kind of business we do.*

*"The reason I'm bringing this up over a dinner meeting
is because we take referrals very seriously and I
wanted to walk you through our process so you get a
clear picture of how we handle referrals and also of
the kind of investors who stand to benefit most from
our services."*

By describing your referral process in some detail, you begin to make the client's fears go away. A signal that this is working might be a question from the client. Questions and other conversational engagement are signs the client is interested and paying attention.

*"First, you need to know how we handle referrals. Whenever a client gives us the name of a friend or colleague, typically what we do is ask the client to make first contact with a letter or an e-mail introducing us to their friend. Then we usually contact them with a letter, or a phone call if you think that would be better. Our goal is only to set up an initial interview, which leads to a more in-depth financial analysis session.*

*"As you know, we never make any recommendations about anything before we've had a chance to listen carefully and review the client's needs and current situation."*

This reduces the risk of you losing their friend's money or the referral coming back to the client after some risky stock idea goes bad.

*"We also might invite them to one of our educational symposiums. You know how much fun those can be.*

*I'm telling you this because I want you to understand the kind of treatment your friends will get from us. You will never be embarrassed by the way we treat your people. All investors are different and your friends will get totally customized service. We never use a 'cookie-cutter' approach. There is too much of that out there and it's just not how we do things. Your friends are going to feel like they've entered a whole new world of personalized financial care...and it will reflect very well on you as the person who referred them."*

Being embarrassed is a major fear top clients have about referrals. Make this go away as quickly as you can and results will follow.

### – Client

*"I'm glad to hear that. It sounds great."*

### – Advisor

*"Naturally we will let you know how things go as the relationship progresses, but even if we don't end up*

*working together, they are going to have a wonderful experience with us and they will probably get a tremendous amount of great information. We want to make sure they report back to you very enthusiastically. The whole process is going to be valuable and enjoyable for them. So you can rest assured in that regard."*

Clients like to know how things are going with the referral...maybe not in detail, but in general terms. So report back and encourage the referral to report back to the client as well. Even if it doesn't work out, the experience will be a great one and a positive report will greatly increase the chances of future referrals from that client!

If, for some bizarre reason the referral doesn't go well...you need to be proactive with the client and let them know that something went wrong.

### – Client

*"That's wonderful, Jim."*

### – Advisor

*"Bob, the second part of our referral process is total confidentiality. At no time will anyone on my team ever discuss your financial interests or investment program with anyone you send us as a referral. That probably goes without saying, but I wanted to assure you of total privacy. I wouldn't want my friends knowing anything about my finances and our top clients feel that way too. In truth, it's very rare that a referral would ever ask, but we absolutely never talk about anything you've done with anyone."*

Confidentiality is a major issue you must address before you can expect them to let you into their inner circle.

### – Client

*"Thanks Jim. I assumed that's how you would handle it."*

### – Advisor

*"Finally...I just wanted to give you a flavor for the kinds of people who might benefit from our services. It might help your thought process when you find yourself talking to a friend."*

This part of the conversation should reflect your actual business model.

*"We love to work with entrepreneurs, professionals like attorneys, physicians, accountants, and architects, and obviously other business-owners like yourself. I am actually very interested in the metals industry, but we can talk about that in a second."*

*"The second group is anyone who is nearing retirement. We have developed an expertise in this area that helps those folks get the safety they want with the income they need...even in a very low interest rate environment."*

Sometimes it's good to cast a broad net for potential referrals. In other cases, where it fits your business model, it might be better to specify a narrow band of clients you prefer to work with. This is especially true if you are building a niche business or trying to target a specific industry group...which would be a great idea, by the way!

*"The third major group is people who might have complicated financial problems like estate issues, a business they're selling, large positions in company stock...that kind of thing. We have many ways to help people in complex situations that other firms simply do not have."*

*"Finally, and this is a broad category, so I will leave it up to your imagination. We want to work with anyone who is tired of getting bad advice, the run-around, and poor service, and generally is unhappy with their current advisor. If you ever run into anyone who gives you this kind of feeling, just let us know about them. We are specialists at restoring damaged confidence*

*and helping people get to their goals conservatively and with consistent discipline."*

*"Because we are being very selective about which clients we ask for referrals from we would be happy to work with anyone you send us. There is not much personal reward in it for you other than my thanks and the knowledge that you would be helping people gain access to what is one of the top financial services teams in the country...which believe it or not...we are."*

**– Client**

*"I'm not surprised."*

**– Advisor**

*"That's nice to hear Bob. We can take a minute now, if you like, and walk through some folks you might have in mind."*

If the client has some names, take this time to obtain as much profile information on their friend or colleague as they are comfortable giving you.

**– Client**

*"Well I really didn't have anyone in mind right now."*

This is where any intelligence work you've done pays off. You're going to prompt him with specific names. Don't make him randomly think of people on his own.

**– Advisor**

*"No problem Bob, I didn't think you would. But if you don't mind...I may have a name for you and I'd love your input. I actually had some interest in working with some of the people in your industry. One name I've been meaning to call for weeks now is Leonard McCoy over at Federated Surgical Supply. He seems like the kind of guy we might like to work with. What do you think?"*

If you don't want to go that route, then simply say...

*"No problem. I didn't expect you would. I just wanted to bring up the subject and also give you a special Referral Guide\* we've prepared for our top clients. It will give you some specific things you can tell anyone about our group. It has a nice article about us and a list of services we provide as well as a few extra business cards in case you want to hand them out at the club or the office. As you can tell, we take referrals very seriously here at First Hungarian...so this is a process to which we have given a lot of thought and energy. It's really the only way we accept new clients."*

### – Client

*"It sounds like you've given this a lot of thought."*

### – Advisor

*"We have Bob. We handle referrals with as much care as possible. They are the only way we accept new relationships and we're very good at them. So do you have any questions I might be able to answer for you?"*

\*The Referral Guide is covered in Referral Strategy #10.

*Referral Strategy #4*

# Stay Top-of-Mind

---

## Concept overview:

- HNW clients are busy people and they're not thinking about you or who to refer to you.

- But every day they are interacting with other people to whom you would love to be referred.

- You need to stay on the client's personal radar screen in positive and creative ways that help them remember you exist and are worthy of referrals.

- This can be fun and great for the relationship as well as for referrals.

---

I live in a suburb of Boston, Massachusetts, called Franklin. It's a nice town and home of the first library in America with books donated by Ben himself! Yes, I know Philadelphia says *they* were first...but they just have better PR.

So one day, I was out looking at my lawn and I ran into a new neighbor who had just moved into the 'hood. We had one of those neighborly moments. *"Hey how are you...welcome to the neighborhood...blah, blah, blah."*

I asked him what he does and he said he's an executive with a biotech company who just got a nice promotion. He'd been in Southern

California for several years but they're originally from Connecticut and are thrilled to be back in the Northeast. He asked what I do and I told him that I'm with a money management firm and I train financial advisors in how to do business.

His eyebrows went up and he said,

> *"That's amazing! I'm actually looking for a good financial advisor right now. My family is selling a big piece of land in Connecticut that we've owned for quite a while and it's a fairly sizeable amount of money. My broker is back in San Diego and I don't think he can help me with this. I'd love someone local...do you know anybody good?"*

The quintessential referral moment!

> *"Of course, you should call my guy...he's fantastic! His name is Tom...ahhh. Tom......"*

BAM — I forgot my advisor's last name!

A hundred names and faces came flooding into my mind and for a critical moment that seemed like forever...I could not remember his name.

> *"Wait right here...I'll get you his card."*

I ran back into the house and started searching for a business card but NO CARDS! I had to go to the website, print out his page and tear off the corner with his name and number. It took me a good eight minutes at least. By the time I got back to my neighbor...the referral was dead! You could see in his eyes that he was not going to call Tom. I blew it. I dropped the ball on the goal line and it sat there like a big awkward egg waiting to hatch and scream, "YOU'RE AN IDIOT!" There I was, this big-time financial expert and I couldn't even come up with the name of a good advisor.

Now who's at fault here?

OK...I own part of it. How could I forget Tom's last name? I've worked with him for years. That was absurd.

But, personally...I blame Tom!

I get nothing from him. I have no letters, no brochures, no research reports, no damn business cards...nothing. When the magic moment came for me to tell his story to a highly qualified prospect...I missed the mark. As good as he is and as much as I wanted to refer him, I am unqualified as a disciple.

Don't let this happen to you. Never let your best people forget you. It's a crime of immense proportions against the success of your business.

## They're not thinking about you!

Remember, you occupy only about two basis points of brain space in the mind of your top clients. They are not thinking about you on any regular basis. This isn't because they don't like you; they're just too busy doing the things they do to be high-net-worth.

Carry this one further step and you will understand that they are also NOT regularly wondering which friends or colleagues they can refer to you. Referrals are not on their mind. You must keep yourself and the idea of referrals in their heads if you want to maximize your referral efforts.

What makes this particularly sad is the fact that every one of your top clients is in a position to refer you to someone every single day! They are mixing and interacting with people all day long with whom you would love to do business. And in many cases they're talking about money and markets or world events. Your name simply does not come up...and that's what we're about to change.

## Stay in touch

So how do you stay top of mind? The simple answer is through frequent contact. Studies have shown that HNW clients like pretty regular contact to the tune of once every two weeks on average. This is a bell curve that centers out around thirty contacts per year. So the once-a-month phone call is at the lowest end of that range. And the number goes up as the value of the portfolio increases. Wealthier clients, on average, like more frequent contact.

The phone is good for quick contact and timely conversations. And, unless you're being taped, your discussion will not end up on a regulator's desk, whereas you should assume that anything you put in writing can and will. So I would continue to use the phone as my base mode of communication if that works for you, but too many advisors stop there.

Check all of these ideas with compliance because you may have restrictions that narrow this list a bit, but in general here are some top-of-mind options you might use:

- **E-mail** – Older clients may not use e-mail but most Baby Boomers and younger clients do. A regular e-newsletter would be a great idea or just a periodic message with an article or research report attached.

- **Newsletters** – There is no law or NASD regulation that prohibits an advisor from writing a newsletter. That said…good luck getting one through compliance. At some firms it doesn't pay to fight this battle. Your better bet may be to use the company's newsletter. Most firms will send your clients one with your name on it. Obviously you cannot control the content of the piece but they're usually pretty good. And the fact that it appears monthly or quarterly with your name on it is the majority of the battle. So use it.

- **Articles you write** – Again, no laws against this but now it might be *worth* the effort to get these approved. An article has a longer shelf life than a newsletter and it elevates the perception of your abilities in the mind of the client. People who write stuff are smarter and better than people who do not. Not always true, but a valid perception nonetheless.

- **Third-party articles** – These would be from magazines, newspapers and the Internet. Again, you may have restrictions on what or how many you can send out, but this is an extremely valuable way to build your business.

  *I once knew a broker in Baltimore named Harry Ford who was recognized on television in a piece entitled "The Best Broker in Town." Part of the show consisted of interviews with Harry's clients and I couldn't wait to hear what they had to say. I expected to hear stories of stock-picking prowess or some kind of market wisdom. Instead they all said one thing in common. "He sends me articles."*

*What made this doubly frustrating was the fact that the articles he sent had very little to do with investing or money. Mostly he sent things that they were interested in. But what genius! Harry was listening to his clients and learning what was important to them. Today, twenty-five years later, this is more commonplace but back then he was ahead of his time. The articles became a proxy for an ethereal process called "paying attention"! Harry had mastered it and reaped the rewards of this simple yet massively successful strategy.*

Now, I am not an expert in copyright laws and I have no desire to steal someone else's intellectual property. It may be illegal to send articles to people or your firm may have some insane Draconian policy against it. So if you find an article that's particularly appealing...send them the whole damn magazine! No one can stop you from doing that.

- **Magazine subscriptions** – This is the next logical step in that progression. But again, what kind of magazines? Stay away from all financial pubs like *Money*, *Fortune* and *Forbes*. I don't want any potential for conflicting financial advice. You want to send something that interests the client. Maybe a magazine about a hobby or a personal passion. Maybe a magazine that will help them in their business like *Harvard Business Review*. My never-fail favorite is *National Geographic*. Besides the outstanding articles and photographs, it's a very classy magazine printed on high-quality paper. And it's something people save for a long time. The shelf life is extraordinary.

  Contact the subscription department and let them know you're sending this as a gift and it will appear with your name on it every month. They also have a new one out called *National Geographic Traveler*, which combines the striking richness of *Nat Geo* with one of the great passions of many HNW clients. And it's cheap, just $19 for a full year's subscription. I would immediately do that for my top fifty clients if I were you.

- **Conference calls** – These are an easy and inexpensive way to deliver an excellent, high-value service to your top clients.

Plus it's extremely comfortable and convenient for people, allowing them to dial in from their own home or office. Imagine hosting a call with ten or twenty of your top clients and a guest speaker who might do a brief update of the markets, a particular theme you've been working on, or an individual investment idea. It's generally better to keep these tactical and short, no more than twenty to thirty minutes with Q&A. If a client calls in from her office, you can have her invite any friends in to listen as well. You might generate some bonus referrals from colleagues who never get this kind of treatment from their advisors.

*"Hey what are you listening to?"*

*"Oh my financial advisor has me on a conference call with an expert on oil and gas drilling."*

*"Really...my advisor never does anything like that for me. Mind if I listen?"*

- **Letters, cards and postcards** – Ironically, in the age of electronics, paper mail is gaining in popularity. People love to get a letter or a postcard that's handwritten and personal. In fact, the personal letter may be the most valuable form of communication you can use. Just think how you feel when you get a handwritten note from someone.

  Sending cards at all the traditional times is good, but pretty common. I'd try to look for uncommon times to celebrate. I like the Fourth of July card that celebrates the birth of the greatest nation on earth. I like the anniversary card...not the client's wedding anniversary, but the anniversary of the start of the client's relationship with you! Hey this is a relationship business, right? So that must be a big day, I'm thinking.

- **Brainsharks** – These are basically web-based seminars with PowerPoint slides and live or recorded audio. They are a great way to combine visual content and audio, which can be helpful when communicating more complex ideas. All you do is send out a URL in an e-mail message and the whole process is automated from there. It's easy and fun and can be viewed at the client's own pace. Contact www.brainshark.com for more information.

- **Gifts** – I've had a lot of luck with gifts over the years and I enjoy giving them. Now, your firm may have restrictions...so learn and obey them. Typically we live in the $100 area, not including tickets to sporting events, theater, or the "occasional" dinner. But for $100, you can find a lot of nice stuff to send your top clients. And after all...what can you get them they don't already have?

  So stick with something creative and thoughtful. I like the gifts that they will look at on a regular basis. One of my personal favorites is antique maps. You can find these easily on eBay. The good ones aren't cheap but then neither are you. Buy one that has special meaning to the client, have it framed, and send it with a note on a special occasion.

- **Events** – We're going to discuss event referrals in a minute but you should have a regular calendar of events set up throughout the year. These can be seminars, golf outings, dinners whatever you like to do to which a client can be invited.

## The forty-four touch system

Overall, a good blend of touches would include most of these items. Your contact plan may look like this:

- - Biweekly phone call (26)

- - Monthly e-mail, newsletter, or magazine (12)

- - Quarterly seminar, dinner, event, or face-to-face meeting (4)

- - Annual client appreciation gathering (1)

- - Special gift (1)

Not including extraordinary situations generated by some market activity or financial situation, this is a total of forty-four touches during the year and that's a great number. Even better, many of them can be automated or are leveraged, which means one event reaches a lot of people simultaneously. This forty-four touch system can be a great model for you. This would almost be the max you can do to stay on my mind without becoming obnoxious. If I don't remember you with this system…chances are I never will.

## *Expand your footprint*

Part of the reason you occupy such a tight space in the client's mind is that you've chosen to pigeonhole yourself into that box. Generally, the only time you interact with the client is when it concerns the portfolio or investing. If all you are is the stock and bond guy or the insurance guy or the mortgage guy…then I'm only going to think of you when one of these specific subjects comes up.

I say break out and expand your connection to the client in ways that go beyond this narrow band of interests. This will help you cast a bigger referral net when the client is talking to friends, colleagues or relatives. What are the issues that most deeply affect your top twenty clients? What are they thinking and talking about to their friends and colleagues all day long? How can you provide any insight or value to those conversations?

Every client is different and you need to do some serious homework to understand their world. But you're on the way to becoming a true partner in my success and that is something I can talk about. Your name is now a lot more likely to come up during the course of my normal day.

*Referral Strategy #5*

# Address The Risks & Emotions of Referrals

## Concept overview:

- Top clients and centers of influence run huge personal and professional risks when referring friends, families, and colleagues.

- Making those risks go away will dramatically increase the number and quality of referrals you get.

- You demonstrate an understanding of risk and fear by discussing them openly and showing in detail how you handle referrals.

- Doing this will greatly increase your referrals and differentiate you from other financial professionals.

When you ask for referrals you're going to hear lots of things similar to this:

> *"I can't think of anyone."*
>
> *"Let me think about it."*
>
> *"I'll get back to you."*
>
> *"Why don't you give me your cards and I'll give them out."*

*"I don't get involved in my friends' finances."*

*"I don't give referrals."*

These are emotional statements masquerading as logical or intellectual arguments. In fact, the whole referral process is filled to the brim with risk for the client and thus it's an extremely emotional process…not a logical one.

What are the clients really saying here? Two things, actually:

1.  I don't trust you.

2.  I'm scared.

It's not that they don't trust you with their money; after all they are your client. But as we discussed in the first chapter, trust comes in many forms and there are three specific levels of trust.

Level one is the basic level where a client trusts you enough to handle a portion of their financial future.

On level two, your relationship has grown to the point that you are the primary advisor for that client. They have placed the bulk of their wealth in your hands.

Level three is the highest and most difficult pinnacle to reach. This is the point at which they are willing to trust you with the most critical people in their lives. This is the "Referral Zone" for HNW clients.

## Unique to HNW clients

Most average clients only go up to level two. This is one of the major differences between HNW and average clients. In the HNW client's world…bringing you into their inner circle of friends, colleagues and relations (level three) is far more difficult and risky than simply giving you their portfolio.

Think about this for a minute. In many cases, the wealth they have created to date (and are still creating) has been acquired through a complex network of business and personal relationships. The people in their world are the source of their success and money. These people represent their future — the business deals yet to be done, the boards yet to be chaired, the companies yet to be taken public.

If you spoil, undermine or damage those relationships for them, you have done far worse than lose them money in a tech fund!  You've potentially hurt their future, which is bigger than their past or present...and that's the critical understanding most financial advisors lack.

For HNW clients...the relationships are a greater risk than the money. And just because you may be really good at managing the money (level two trust) does not mean you would be good at handling those critical relationships.

So when a HNW client says, "I can't think of anyone," what they're really saying is...

*"I cannot think of anyone that I would trust you to handle yet that would not come back to bite me in the butt or hurt my future in some meaningful way if you royally screwed something up for them. So I'd rather not deal with the whole issue at the moment thank you very much!"*

## What about fear?

Obviously, trust and fear are tied together. HNW clients have several overlapping fears when it comes to referrals. They vary in intensity and priority, but they're usually all present to some degree.

Once again...they cannot say, "I'm scared." So they say all those other things. Fear is the hidden objection — the one you cannot solve until it's out in the open. Getting it out is tricky, but first let's understand what the fears might be.

### Fear of risking their relationships

Clients worry that if they give you the name of a friend or colleague, you might do something that could jeopardize their relationship with that person.

Who *knows* what you might do? There are a million possibilities that come to the client's mind. You might lose the friend's money, provide bad advice, bad service, fail to meet some obligation...something that could potentially come back to reflect badly on the client.

No one wants to hear, *"Hey Bob, that financial planner you gave my number to is a real jerk! You know what he did?..."* That's a potential nightmare in today's minimal-contact society.

If you doubt this relationship risk...just imagine your own personal situation for a second. I'm your financial advisor. You have a next door neighbor...Jim. You give me Jim's name as a referral and I call him. What's the absolute BEST thing that can happen to YOU as a result of giving me that referral to Jim?

The best-case scenario is that Jim leans over the fence one summer afternoon and says,

> *"Hey (your name here)! Thanks for having that guy call me! He's really great and he's helped us out a lot. I really appreciate that buddy...thanks!"*

That's it...the maximum upside — the over-the-hedge Thank You!

What's the maximum downside?

> *"Hey (your name here)! Do me a favor, will you? Lose my phone number! That guy you told to call me is the biggest pain in the ass I've ever seen. He's been calling every night for a month...right at dinner time and he's woken up the baby three times. He's becoming a real nuisance. Don't EVER give my phone number out to anyone else...OK?"*

Pretty bad! If a neighbor ever said that to me I'd be planting some serious trees on the property line but quick!

But it gets worse:

> *"Hey (your name here)! That guy you turned loose on me last year lost five hundred grand in my IRA. You'll be hearing from my attorney...I just wanted you to know what a disaster you caused."*

Impossible, you say? Not in today's world...I guarantee it.

Always remember that for a HNW client, referrals are like writing naked call options. The upside is extremely small and the downside is virtually unlimited. You are asking them to expose themselves to significant danger for very little personal benefit. And in case you were wondering...making you happy or helping you grow your business is not enough of a benefit to overcome that fear.

## Fear of sharing personal information

Your client doesn't want any of their friends and neighbors to know anything about their financial situation. People today are extremely private about personal matters involving money and insurance...unless they're bragging about some hot-performing thing they bought, which usually only happens in Beverly Hills.

Clients fear that you will divulge some secret about them in order to convince the referral to do business. Their nightmare looks like this:

> *"Hello Bob, my name is Jim Tentpeg with First Hungarian. One of your colleagues, George Thompson, happens to be a client of mine and he asked me to give you a call regarding our new insurance services. I don't know if you realize just how difficult it's been to insure old George...what with the heart attacks, the strokes and the sexually transmitted diseases...but he thought I might be able to help you."*

Now that's certainly absurd...but clients fear it nonetheless. They pretty much figure you would throw them under a bus in order to do business with the referral.

The second part of this privacy issue is a bit more convoluted, but equally important to understand in today's society.

I don't want my neighbor thinking about my money. And I don't want him thinking that I am thinking about *his* money. Basically the subject of finances falls under a broad social contract we have that says, *"I mind my own business...you mind yours!"*

The risk to the client is that their friend might think,

> *"Hey, I wonder why George asked this guy to call me. Doesn't he think that I'm as successful as he is? Maybe my wife leaked out about the losses we took in the portfolio last summer. What else has she been telling her friends at those garden club meetings?"*

Or better...

*"That George is so cocky. He's always bragging about his market successes. He actually thinks I would use his advisor. He must be crazy."*

Frankly, it's a lot easier to just avoid the whole referral process altogether.

## Fear of how you will handle the referral

What are you going to do when I give you the name of a friend or colleague? Are you going to handle them carefully, professionally with extreme sensitivity, and make them feel very good? Or will you call them every night at dinnertime for six weeks and annoy the hell out of them like you did to me? Are you going to embarrass me in some way?

This is a particular danger if you've been overly aggressive in the handling of the client in the first place. The client imagines that you will do the same thing to their friend. And while they might have been willing to put up with it…they are not about to knowingly subject a friend to that sales pressure. It's hard to say to a client, *"I may have been obnoxious and pushy with you, but I won't be with your referrals."*

This "handling" issue also touches on the important area of your personal style.

Remember that referrals are not about your firm or your product…but about you personally. I may like you well enough to let you handle my money, but there may be some aspects of your personality or behavior that I would not want to turn loose on my "inner circle." In fact, I may not even want my friends knowing that I work with you.

There could be a hundred subtle and subjective reasons for the way I feel, but you may never know about them because I have accepted you. Those characteristics are no longer annoying to me, but they do become a concern in the context of other people.

*I had a custom clothing guy back in Los Angeles who did some fantastic suits and shirts for me. He was a very nice guy, knew his profession, and I loved his suits. He came to my office and measured me (with the big tape) and did a very professional job. The suits and shirts came back perfect and they were really wonderful products.*

*This fellow always asked me for referrals to others in my office. He figured that I probably knew a few people who also liked custom suits...and he was right. My boss was an ideal candidate...as were a few of my brokers. But there was something about this guy to which I did not want to expose my friends.*

*He had the world's worst bad breath. We are talking a stinking draft from a slaughterhouse kind of breath. A battalion of Tic Tacs would commit suicide before going into that battle. You get the idea.*

*I learned to deal with it and breathe around it. So I should have been willing to refer him...and yet I was not. Does that make me a bad person? I suppose if I really cared I would have told him, but I only saw him twice a year and I really didn't want to embarrass him or rock the boat. It was easier to blow off the whole referral subject.*

Now, you may say that's not a valid comparison because he was not as important to me as a financial advisor is to a HNW client. Yet I spent many thousands of dollars with him and dealt with his products every single day of my life! So from a sheer exposure standpoint, I thought about this guy twenty times more frequently than any other professional in my world.

The point is there may be something about you that makes referring you a frightening act for the client. Why not try a simple personal style survey and ask yourself,

- Am I the kind of person that can mix well with the inner circles of my best clients?

- Are my personal attributes (appearance, behavior, speech, sense of humor, social skills, personality, grooming, etc.) consistent with a professional image at the level of the client and their associates?

These are tough issues to deal with and we certainly all have our personal flaws. I have several items myself that keep me out of the top levels in my own world and I am very aware of them. Knowing and changing are totally different things, by the way.

Total honesty is crucial for your success. And if you are not sure...then get help from a trusted mentor. Friends may not be brutal enough with you and they've already accepted your flaws...so bringing them into the spotlight, even to help you, may not be something they want to do.

Finally, and without making this subject overly complicated: you need to view this issue of compatible personal styles in the light of the client's relationship with their inner circle...not only with you. Clients may have a certain way of interacting with you that leads you to conclude they are happy and comfortable with your relationship and obviously willing to refer you. But they may not behave the same way with their friends, colleagues, and critical relationships.

As intelligent human beings, we have a certain innate ability to present various faces to the different people in our world at different times. They come to know us a certain way and to alter that presentation may not be in our best interests. The client/advisor relationship can take many forms that simply would not work in other relationships.

For example, a client may appear to you to be a bold risk-taker and a Devil-may-care bon vivant. That may be a facet of their personality they choose to portray with you for a variety of reasons. It's how they want you to see them and it serves the relationship in some way to do so. It may not be how their family, friends or colleagues see them. So opening up that world to you might jeopardize the image they have cultivated in your mind. *"I don't want you to know that I'm really a wimp!"*

## Referrals from other professionals

If you are seeking referrals from another professional like an accountant or an attorney...you have another layer of fear to overcome. Now a referral screw-up by you means they lose years of direct income from their client! This is why most "peripheral professionals" are notoriously stingy with referrals until they really get comfortable with you.

By the way, many if not all of these fears may eventually go away on their own over time. It's certainly true that once you've built a bond of trust and the client has years of positive experience with you as their advisor, they are much more willing to give referrals. I'm not suggesting that these fears will stand in your way forever.

But why wait? You can do things early in the relationship to accelerate the process of getting referrals from your top clients. This pushes your own business growth curve far to the left and could take years off your business plan!

## *These fears seem unrealistic*

Sure...maybe...to you! Please understand that these fears are real whether *you* think they are or not. This is not a question of what you think is legitimate, logical or reasonable. Fears do not have to be reasonable...that's why they're *fears*. Don't get wrapped around the axle trying to justify an emotion; you cannot. All you can do is understand it and try to deal with it in the most effective manner possible.

## *Overcoming the fears*

### Step 1: Talk about the risk.

What type of professional tells the cons as well as the pros of a given recommendation? Only someone who is totally confident in their ability and professional skill. So be that person.

Bring up the subject of referral risk first...before the thought even enters the client's head. Hit it directly and don't hide from it. By doing so, you are distinguishing yourself from every other advisor in the client's world. Try inserting this conversational segment into the later half of the Strength Referral message from Chapter 7.

#### – You

*"Bob...since we're talking about referrals, I just want you to understand that we know there is a certain amount of risk in the referral process for you...and I want to be absolutely clear how we will handle this so you know the pros and cons up front.*

*"The upside is you get to help someone you care deeply about. And we can help...that's pretty much assured."*

*"But the downside is that if we were to somehow screw up ...you might lose a friend. This understanding is foremost on our minds whenever we handle referrals for our top clients."*

## Step 2: Show how you handle this risk.

*"Bob...that's why **we try never to take any risks with a new referral.** We want their first experiences with our team to be straight down the middle of the fairway...very positive and solid investment experiences. What we want is for them to come back to you and say, **'Hey those guys are FANTASTIC! I wish you told me about them earlier?'"***

*"Our recommendations to a new referral are always based on an extremely detailed financial planning process and high-quality investments. You know how thorough we tend to be. We never deal in speculative or dangerous investment ideas. That's just not the way we do business. We simply do not let our people take excessive risk with their money."*

## Step 3: Tell them the benefits of your approach.

*"The benefit of this conservative strategy is that it gives our clients a tremendous comfort level about the referral process. They know that we would never do anything that might cause harm to their relationships and they can be assured that their friends are getting the very best care possible."*

## Step 4: Blow your own horn *(optional).*

*"Frankly, that's one of the reasons my team and I have been so successful. We get more referrals from our clients than anyone else in town. [No official stats are kept, but this sounds great to me.] This blue-chip referral approach works not only for our top clients but it just makes great business sense as well."*

That whole conversation add-on took less than a minute and it set you up as a serious professional who has given a great deal of thought to the referral process.

Is this a more difficult conversation to have with a client? Well let's consider one alternative. This is a very popular technique currently being taught all around the industry and it's PURE STUPIDITY!

### – YOU

*"So Bob...anyone else you know who might be interested in this Super Duper Growth Fund?"*

### – CLIENT

*"Hmmm....I honestly can't think of anyone."*

### – YOU

*"Well Bob, do you mind if I help you? Let's brainstorm a bit. How about people you drive to work with...people you pass on the way to work...people you actually work with? How about your doctor, your attorney, your golf buddies? Who painted your house? Who details your car? Who's your vet?"*

And on you go with that inane litany of possible relationships...none of which you are going to get close to.

Instead of realizing that the client is dealing with an emotional issue involving trust and fear, you're going to try to help them think of someone...because obviously they're morons and having trouble coming up with names. What you're really doing is giving them new and improved ways to be afraid. Let's just spread that referral risk to every person in your world! So stop doing that, please.

## Why not wait?

The idea of bringing up fears and risks in advance of the client may seem odd to you. Why not simply wait to see if the objection comes up naturally? Why inject fear into the conversation if it's not there?

What I am telling you is that it IS there whether you are aware of it or not. In the mind of the HNW client — the clients to whom this entire referral approach has been specifically targeted — that risk is always present...and they will never say anything about it to you. It's just not the way they deal with this issue.

That's not true about all your clients. Those basic clients for whom level two trust is the top rung on the ladder do not require this approach. In fact, if you were to talk to them about risks and fears, you might scare the crap out of them. All they need to prompt a referral might be the simple, "Who else do you know...?"

But those clients are not our concern...remember?

With HNW clients, being proactive in your disclosure about this feeling they have bumps you up several notches in their mind. Now you might actually deserve to be in that inner circle. Anyone with this level of awareness and self-confidence — who understands my fears yet who deals with them so honestly — certainly is worth a shot.

*Referral Strategy #6*

# Target a Specific Industry or Client Niche

## Concept overview:

- Specializing in a certain industry or a type of client can dramatically increase your referrals from those groups.

- The goal of becoming the "go to" advisor for an entire industry can be a major career driver with benefits that go far beyond referrals.

- Selecting an industry or client group to target is a simple process that can be replicated for scalable business results.

One of the most powerful business-building strategies you can engage in is called industry target marketing (ITM). This is a concept that can have huge long-term rewards for your business in addition to generating tremendous referrals.

The goal of ITM is to own a significant chunk of an entire industry or profession within your community, your region, or even the country. With ITM you become the "go to" advisor for an entire group of folks who all have a lot of money and a lot in common. They are a homogenous demographic and psychographic group.

There are thousands of examples of groups you might want to target and each region of the country has certain industries that may be particularly prominent or identifiable. For example, you wouldn't go to Green Bay, Wisconsin if you wanted to target stage and screen actors. That would be Los Angeles or New York City. Boston is a great place for the medical and bio-tech world. Gaming industry professionals are concentrated in Las Vegas, Atlantic City and Mississippi.

These are the obvious examples, but the real money will be made in the more hidden gems. Groups like video post-production professionals or one of my favorites, custom home builders. Every part of the country has high-end home builders who make a boatload of money and who would benefit from your services.

We are talking about something very specific. I get a kick out of advisors who tell me they like to work with "corporate executives" or "business owners." Why not just say "higher vertebrates" and really open things up? Those are not niches. "Doctors" is also too wide a range. Tell me orthodontists or urologists and now you have a niche. The narrower you get, the more likely you will be to get a buzz going in that community. You can always expand later.

## *Which industry to target?*

There are six keys to selecting a good target industry:

### 1. Find an industry that has money.

Look for a group of strong local or regional businesses with an entrepreneurial mentality and wealthy folks at various levels. Don't stop at the obvious choices. For example, every financial advisor targets doctors at some point in their career. But you can dig deeper. Chances are that there may be some medical specialty that has a particular concentration in your region. Find out what the local teaching hospitals are really good at and talk to as many health care professionals as you know. It might be something virtually unknown or unrecognized except to professionals in the medical community.

Think outside the box. There are many hidden industries that have a lot of wealthy folks but that no one knows anything about. You may have one right next door or pass several on the way to work. Keep your eyes open and ask questions.

*Recently I had some landscaping done in my back yard. We put in a nice pool, a couple of stone walls, decking, trees, etc. It was quite a project. One day while looking over the cost estimates for the stone work...it struck me that I was paying a lot of money for stupid rocks that seem to grow wild in my New England yard. I started to get curious about where all this money was going so I decided to dig deeper (no pun intended).*

*I paid a visit to the local rock place. I think they called it the "landscape design center." I drove in and saw this snazzy showroom that looked like a new car dealership in front of a giant arena the size of 10 football fields filled with different types of rocks, bricks, pavers, boulders and pebbles. Huge trucks and dozers and front-end loaders were crawling all over this place and it was quite an impressive scene. Up until that moment I had no idea this was happening less than 5 minutes from my home.*

*I walked into the showroom, which was beautifully designed, and struck up a conversation with the manager. It was a slow weekday morning and he seemed happy to chat. Long story short — I come to learn that this business is booming all over the country. He told me that his company was adding five new locations even bigger than this one in the northeast and they still can't keep up with the demand. The money was huge and they had only begun to tap the real market potential.*

*Bamn...just like that I uncovered a massive target industry. Who the hell knew anything about rocks? Not me! But evidently there's big money in them stones and most of the business are privately held mom and pop shops that have grown tremendously in the past few years with the building and renovation boom.*

*Oh, that was another thing he said — new construction was less than half their business! The big money was in renovation which was a lot more resistant to recessions and a potential housing bubble. Sweet!*

*I left there thinking that if I were still a broker I would be all over this industry like salt on a peanut. The billionaire next door?*

*You're damn right baby! They are all around us and many are not being prospected by anyone.*

## 2. Find an industry that intrigues you personally.

You want to work with a group of people whom you respect and in a field that you would like to learn more about because you are going to be immersing yourself in it. If it's boring to you, the job of becoming an insider may be emotionally impossible for you.

Pick something that's intellectually stimulating to you. I assume that you have interests outside of the financial world. Maybe you love music or theater or arts. Maybe you have a hobby that you really enjoy. Is there an industry associated with that hobby that might have some money in it?

Chances are pretty good that some activity you love to do is attached somehow to money. You just need to look at it from multiple angles and find the hidden connections. An example of a hidden connection might be golf. Maybe you love the game and think there's a lot of money to be made targeting golf pros at the country clubs in your area. It's worth exploring but it may turn out to not be as true as you hoped. But how about the golf equipment wholesalers who sell stuff to those country clubs. Just like our industry has wholesalers for mutual funds, annuities and managed money...every other industry has them too. And you will never meet them unless you dig and do your research.

## 3. Your previous career

Many advisors today have come into this business from another career and have a professional background and contacts that can be mined for referrals. That would be a natural place to start your industry target marketing campaign, assuming it meets some of the other criteria. But use caution here.

I strongly recommend to new advisors that they avoid prospecting their old colleagues for at least one or two years after they get started. I know that others may tell you differently; they want you to go right after all those old buddies and hit them hard out of the gate...but hear me out.

Let's say you call your old friend back at Acme Widget and proudly announce that you're now a financial advisor with First Hungarian. You may pitch him an idea or try to get together for dinner. What does he know about that impending interaction?

A.    You are new to the financial industry and you cannot possibly know anything about managing money yet. At least not enough to help him and maybe you might even do some damage.

B.    You're trying hard to get started in your new career and your manager probably told you to start by prospecting all your old friends from the widget business.

C.    You are going to use the weight of your previous relationship with him to at least mildly pressure him into doing business. That's going to make him very uncomfortable at best.

In short, he may not be too eager to come to dinner. So the tension mounts, he doesn't return your calls and pretty soon you've damaged or weakened all the great contacts you had in your last industry.

Don't do that! Instead think from the client's perspective first. Far better to send a personalized letter that says something like this:

*Dear Bob,*

*It's been too long since we've spoken and I wanted to drop you a line to update you on my new mission in life.*

*You may have heard that I left Acme Widget last year to become a Financial Advisor with First Hungarian. It's true...I made the leap into the financial industry and I'm having the time of my life! The people I've met at this firm are both brilliant and very professional. I couldn't have picked a better firm.*

*I have spent the past year amassing all the knowledge I can about money and investing. It's been a steep learning curve but I finally "graduated" and am now a fully licensed and registered representative of the New York Stock Exchange and the NASDAQ market. I couldn't be more proud and excited.*

*As one of my oldest friends and professional colleagues...I just want you to know that I am here for you if you need me. If you ever find yourself confused about the markets or just would like an impartial second opinion on something you might be considering with another advisor, please feel free to call me anytime. I don't pretend to have all the answers, but I do have quite a few and I know where to get the rest.*

*In today's confusing world of money it can be a nice feeling to have a trusted friend who knows and cares about you and your family on this side of the investing business. That would be me!*

*Please say "Hi" to all the gang over at ACME. Maybe we can all go to lunch sometime and catch up.*

*All the best!*

*Jim*

*P.S. I am putting together a special advisory board of some former business associates. I'd like to invite you to be a member. We can talk more in a few weeks...but I would value your input and we will have a great dinner.*

That strikes me as a better way to phrase your approach. The old-school way of leaping immediately on your former friends and colleagues to do business is absurd to me. Some insurance companies are notorious for this. They hire a young agent, pressure them to sign up all their relatives, friends and former colleagues as fast as possible, and then keep the accounts when they inevitably run out of people to tap. Not a model for success in the new industry. So be smarter and think like a professional.

## 4. Find an industry cluster.

A cluster is a group of related industries or professionals that all work with each other in some way. Look for an industry that has multiple companies in the area so you can cross-pollinate between them. Custom home builders are a great example here. They touch several HNW related industries like subcontractors, plumbers, electricians, landscapers, equipment sales and rental companies, realtors, bankers, accountants, architects, and even HNW buyers themselves. They are even somewhat recession proof because they can cross over into the home improvement arena when housing takes that inevitable downturn.

Anesthesiologists and radiologists are good examples of a cluster profession in the medical world. They touch many different types of physicians all of whom may be a separate nice in their own right.

## 5. Look toward your favorite clients.

Select an industry in which you already have one or more top clients. This will make it easier to get information and generate initial connections. By talking with the client, you might be able to finagle an invitation to a local industry event and get some of the more popular and widely-read publications to study.

Sit down with your client and talk about their industry concerns and the issues they may be facing. Get a historical perspective on the major trends that have impacted their world. Remember, your goal is to become an insider and that means you're going to need to learn a lot. Some of that information may not lead directly to a sales process. That's OK. Your curiosity must be genuine. If your interest is purely for sales purposes, the people in a position to help you will likely see through your motives very quickly and lock you out. No one said this was going to be easy. Nothing that leads to real success is.

## 6. Find a group you can write for.

Target an industry or professional group that has a regular publication that accepts articles from outside experts. Some groups may have simple newsletters that are designed and published in-house by a member of the group. Others may have a full-blown monthly trade magazine.

The editors of these publications are always looking for interesting content, but they may reject a sales-oriented approach. Keep it educational, informative, and targeted toward their readers. If you're good, you may be able to write a regular column. That may seem like a nightmare...and it's not easy, but the rewards of being a regular are worth the effort.

I used to write a column called *Maselli on the Market* for a weekly newspaper in the town that I was targeting. Making deadlines was always a challenge for me, but content was never a problem. Whenever I got stuck for an idea I would simply do a Q&A column where I answered reader questions on certain issues.

Admittedly, that would be very hard to do in today's restrictive regulatory environment. But writing a column is absolutely NOT illegal so be prepared to make your case point intelligently with a business plan and manager support. And keep in mind that an editor may want to see several completed articles before agreeing to any kind of regular feature. So you may need to go to compliance with six articles for approval in advance of publication.

Look locally to smaller groups as well. For example, my wife runs the local book club in our neighborhood. She writes a monthly newsletter that goes to all the members and she's always looking for interesting content. A  financial advisor who would e-mail her a monthly review of the best finance and investing books would be featured prominently in that piece which reaches a nice demographic. Multiply that by a hundred book clubs in the Boston area and you have a major networking opportunity that would cost you zero money.

## 7. Find a group you can speak to.

Look for a group that comes together in meetings at which you might be able to speak. Most groups have national or regional conventions of some kind. You would be stunned to know how many high-net-worth groups are meeting every week at your city's various convention centers and hotels. These groups aren't marketed to because no financial professionals even think about them.

*When I was a stockbroker in Baltimore a million years ago, I used to travel to Annapolis almost every weekend. This charming town on the shores of the Chesapeake Bay is the sailing capital of the world. The beauty was impressive, but beyond that, I was always struck by the massive amounts of floating capital. It seemed to me that people with big boats were rich and I wanted them as clients.*

*So I rented a booth at the Annapolis Boat Show. I was the only financial professional at the show and the other brokers in my office thought I was nuts. Sure, not everyone was a millionaire but you couldn't swing a whisker pole without hitting a good prospect.*

*For three solid days at my booth I fielded questions from bemused boat buyers... "What are you doing here?" My answer was usually, "I came here to find you!" I left with hundreds of HNW prospects and developed an understanding of the language and concerns of boat owners. Up till then the only boat*

*I had ever been on was the Staten Island Ferry...so this made me an "expert" in the needs of boat owners and got me more than a few invitations to sail the Chesapeake Bay with members of my target audience.*

I understand from some advisors today that this boat show is now over-prospected. They say the only visitors they get are from other advisors. That seems hard to imagine, but it does say something about being early. Take an idea that you believe in...run it by everyone in your office and hope they all say it's crazy and won't work. Then do it! Being totally alone and isolated from the crowd is often a very good sign of potential success.

## Read Dr. Tom Stanley's work

In truth, Industry Target Marketing is a book by itself. Fortunately, that book has already been written by Dr. Tom Stanley. It's called *Marketing to the Affluent* and you should read it (and all his work) from cover to cover.

Being an industry insider makes it a lot easier to get referrals. By knowing the people, their specific needs, concerns, and problems, you can be of much greater value to them. When they talk to each other, your name will come up. Assuming you do good work, you can expand your presence into the group very quickly.

As you will read in Tom Stanley's book, however, becoming an industry insider is a detailed, time-consuming process that takes work and effort. Very often, much of the work you do will not result in any immediate business for you! That knocks about 75% of financial advisors out of the equation. Groups with serious money have seen hundreds of quick-hit privateers come and go. If you embark on this approach solely for your own financial needs, chances are they won't let you anywhere near the center of power or influence.

If, however, you have the tenacity and professional staying power, this can become the greatest business-building strategy you will ever use.

## Start within your own book

Let's imagine you have a current client in an industry that meets the criteria we outlined earlier. The next step is to do some research on that group and learn something about it that you can use to have a conversation with that client.

### – Advisor

*"Hey Bob, I was reading in* Stone World *magazine the other day your industry is in the midst of a massive consolidation of granite quarries worldwide. It's causing huge supply problems for certain very popular types of dimension stone and may be driving up prices. I was wondering how this might be affecting you and your company."*

### – Client

*"What are you doing reading Stone World?"*

### – Advisor

*"I try to keep up with the industry happenings of all my top clients. It gives me some insights into their world and ways I can help them. Besides...I am building a specialty working with professionals in the dimension stone\* and aggregate\* industry. It's a personal passion of mine."*

*(\*Two insider terms)*

OK, first of all, what *are* you doing reading *Stone World* magazine? Well, if you have clients in the rock business that's their industry publication of choice. By reading it, you climbed a few notches in the client's mind. You are now something more than an investment guy trying to sell financial products. You actually care about the client's world.

Just reading the damn magazine may be enough to boost your bird-dog referrals all by itself! The next time the client is in a position to refer your services, guess what he's going to say about you?

*"Larry, you really need to work with Jim. He really understands our world."*

But let's carry this further. Suppose you uncover a trend or a development in the industry that really does concern the client...what can you do about it? Well you could do anything from facilitate a discussion group among local owners to sponsoring a symposium to discuss the concerns with industry leaders to organizing a letter-writing campaign to Congress on their behalf (Tom Stanley's idea).

At this point, your actions are limited only by your own creativity and resources. At the very least, I would host a dinner meeting and invite the other stone guys from the area to discuss their needs and how my firm could help their industry. All of this legitimately falls under the heading of "special services you provide your top clients." The other owners in the room will be wondering why their financial guy doesn't read *Stone World*. You are on your way to true differentiation.

## *Using press to market to your niche*

I am a big believer in the power of the press as a way to generate target market awareness. Getting your profile article in the Boston Globe might be hard. Getting an article in Sporting Clays Magazine might be a bit easier. There needs to be the right angle, but maybe you're sponsoring a local clays tournament to support a charity. Have a photographer take some good pictures and do up a pitch letter to the editor or even a simple press release. Make a contact on the magazine's staff and invite them to attend.

Better yet, do some homework and write a piece on buying antique shotguns as an investment strategy. How *have* top-quality shotguns appreciated over the years and what kind of returns make this a viable investment? Some stories I've heard at the club are quite remarkable.

The older models of some fine guns start at $50,000 and go up from there. At those prices, a few Purdys, Perazzis and Kreighoffs can add up to a potentially non-correlated asset class that might add some alpha to a client's portfolio. It may be just as valid a strategy as collecting old masters, antique cars or Disney cells. There's an article in there somewhere and if you write it you're on your way to becoming an insider.

### Write it yourself

If you did have an article appear

## *Home Builder of the Year*

A few years ago I worked with a financial planning firm that wanted to target the home-builder industry in each of their markets. For the reasons I mentioned earlier, home builders are a fantastic group to prospect.

One of the ideas we came up with was to sponsor a Home Builder of the Year award in each distinct market area. The planner firm put together a survey that they took to the major local realtors. The survey asked them to rate the local home builders in a number of categories such as Best Use of Space, or Most Environmentally Friendly. The idea was to have enough categories so that almost all of the top home builders could be nominated — like Hollywood and the Oscars.

Then the planner firm personally interviewed all the home builders that had been nominated by the realtors. This put them in front of dozens of top prospects in a very unique way. In these interviews, they learned tremendous amounts of detailed information. Often, conversations that started about purely home-building subjects turned personal and a nice level of rapport was reached by the nominated builder and the interviewing planner.

Some of the builders were initially skeptical. What is a financial planning firm doing sponsoring a Home Builder of the Year award? This allowed them to talk about their commitment to the community and how they recognized and appreciated the tremendous contribution home builders make to the health of the community in so many ways, from job creation to attracting upscale buyers and expanding the tax base. Not only is all of this true, but it made the owners feel great to be recognized for doing good work.

Then, as a final grand gesture, the planner firm sponsored a Home Builder of the Year awards dinner complete with press coverage in each local community. These were upscale events that cost some money, but the end result of this process was a wonder to behold.

In little more than two years (virtually no time at all), this planner firm went from being a nobody with no connections to anyone in the group to being the prime insider of the entire industry in each community they targeted. They ultimately owned a good chunk of the industry.

Every custom home builder knew who they were and well over 50% were doing business with the planner firm!

My point is that you can do this too! Whether you're a one-person shop or part of a major firm, you can do the same thing in a scaled-up or down version. There is nothing stopping you except the will to do it and the specific details of implementation, which you can learn.

*Referral Strategy #7*

# Tell Your Story Boldly

## Concept overview:

- The financial services industry is a crowded place with many "advisors" prospecting the same HNW clients.

- Clients have trouble understanding what makes you special and different from your competitors.

- Building a brand identity, developing a compelling story, and learning to tell it well can make all the difference in your marketing and referral effort.

- Your story won't get you any referrals unless the client can tell it to their friends. So build it for them to share.

Branding is a fairly complex issue in the financial services industry and it has several moving parts, including you, your firm, the investment idea or product, and the industry as a whole. All of these actors play a role in the branding drama and their performances have a major impact on your ability to generate referrals from HNW clients. You need to carefully script this play to make it appeal to your different audiences.

Many books have been written on the subject of branding and the topic is all the rage at conferences and meetings. For our purposes, I'm going to keep this simple because I think folks have overcomplicated the concept to the point of confusion.

## *What is my brand?*

Your brand is the image you create in the marketplace. It's something that clients associate with you — a mental picture, a story, a phrase, a product, an experience, or a feeling that pops into their head when your name comes up. It's what you stand for from the *client's* perspective. For referral purposes, it helps them form the message they would tell their friend or colleague about you as an encouragement to call you.

An easy way to think about branding imagery is with this list of popular cars. What's the first thought that pops into your head when you read them? Read down Column 1 and match each car with the popular branding image in Column 2.

| Car | Image |
|---|---|
| A. Chevrolet Corvette | _____ Soccer moms |
| B. Mercedes S500 | _____ Engineering |
| C. GMC Truck | _____ Safety |
| D. Chrysler Minivan | _____ Expensive toy |
| E. Subaru Outback | _____ All-American |
| F. Volvo anything | _____ Reliability |
| G. BMW 750 | _____ Strong |
| H. Porsche convertible | _____ Tree hugger |
| I. Toyota Camry | _____ Luxury |

If you're like most people in my informal survey, you probably listed them as follows:

D, G, F, H, A, I, C, E, B

Brands work for more than just companies and individuals. They can apply to countries as well. One of my favorite old jokes has to do with brand identity on a global level. You've heard this:

*Heaven is a place where... the lovers are Italian, the cooks are French, the mechanics are German, the police are English, and it's all run by the Swiss.*

*Hell is a place where...the lovers are Swiss, the cooks are English, the mechanics are French, the police are German, and it's all run by the Italians.*

# How is a brand communicated?

A brand is communicated in many ways to your clients. Your firm may do advertising. You might use printed materials like marketing brochures, seminar invitations, newsletters, and statements. You also have electronic media like your website. Articles and press coverage contribute major elements to the branding message.

All of these are important, but when it comes to building an identity in the mind of the client or prospect...nothing tops the actual experiences the client has with you and your team.

These experiences or touches can be face-to-face interactions, telephone conversations, group events, personal letters, and e-mails. Such activities form the core of your "touch arsenal" and all together they add up to roughly forty opportunities per year to deliver your brand message and tell your story.

When you consider the millions of sales and branding impressions we receive every year...forty is not a very big number. That means you must maximize the impact of each one for it to build a lasting brand impression. Each message must repeat the core elements of your brand and each touch should involve certain common experiences that reinforce your messaging. It's all tied together into a unified approach aimed at defining who you are or who you want to be for the client — and ultimately what you want the client to tell a potential referral.

On the negative side, all the advertising in the world cannot overcome a bad personal experience. Personal interactions outweigh words by twenty to one, which is one of the reasons referrals are so powerful. When your client tells their friend that you're a great guy, the friend is hearing the results of actions and experiences...not just words. A referral gives them a much closer connection to reality than any marketing campaign ever could.

## *The firm's brand or yours?*

These may be slightly different things and that's OK. Most top advisors are doing quite a bit of their own branding with clients. While their messaging is aligned with the company's story (compliance will make sure of that), it tends to go beyond the company toward a more customized process.

In my experience, it is not uncommon for a top advisor to say something like, *"This is how my company does things…and that's great. But then we go a couple of steps further for our clients."* The reality I've seen is that most clients think of you as more important than the firm. They want to know you work with a good company, but at the end of the day…it's you who will get them to their goals. So a little branding divergence is a good thing.

On the other hand, if you work for a major firm, they're probably spending millions every year in an effort to get their story out there. So it makes some sense to align yourself with the big picture.

You've seen these ads. Your manager will roll out the new ad campaign at the January kick-off meeting. There's music and beautiful imagery and the voice-over is a booming baritone filled with trust and wisdom. Everyone applauds and cheers. Maybe you've secured some prime Super Bowl ad space somewhere between the Budweiser Clydesdales and the Victoria's Secret Halftime Lingerie show. You can just hear the phones ringing!

Look, we can debate the effectiveness of mass market branding at a later date. Suffice to say that the client will make some interim judgments about you by your company's public messaging…until they get to know you. Then, mercifully, it fades away.

> *My personal pick for best recent TV ads is Morgan Stanley. These are the ones that position the Morgan Stanley rep as an important part of a family's life. The one I love most is the beach scene where a wife and husband are talking wistfully about their dream retirement…and then the camera pulls back to reveal that the man talking wasn't the husband at all, but the Morgan Stanley advisor who had become so totally*

*integrated and involved in the couple's future that he was part of the family.*

*Of course, the humor possibilities of that concept were endless and immediately apparent to the folks at Saturday Night Live who did a hysterical spoof of that ad. I see that as evidence that you've hit a major branding chord, but evidently Morgan didn't agree. I heard recently they fired their ad agency. Maybe the message wasn't what they wanted to convey. It certainly was memorable and had impact.*

Public messaging is not always positive. Sometimes your brand can be affected by big picture missteps that broadly undermine investor confidence and trust. Many advisors have seen good relationships turn sour not because of anything they did personally, but because their firm was in the news every day with some scandal or regulatory issue.

Clients have a limited threshold for those kinds of shenanigans...and many will wonder why the hell you are still at a firm that does things in such a perceived shady way. I'm sure some of you have gotten those calls over the past few years. They're no fun. But the good news is that for the most part, clients think of you as the brand. The big firm picture is secondary. So the place to focus your branding effort is on you.

## Building your brand

What do you want the client to think and feel about you? What would you like your message to be and how can you build that message into everything you say and do to reinforce the brand? The best place to begin is with something called a **"Total Truth Assessment."**

This is a careful analysis of who you are — your team's strengths, weaknesses, passions and skills. The goal is to cut through the fluff and the boilerplate and get to the core of what you really do for people that's valuable. A brand that is built on anything other than the organization's deepest truths will most certainly fail.

So what is the truth? Who and what are you? How do you know? What do you bring to the table that makes you compelling and distinguishes you from the hundreds of other advisors who want to help me with my money? This analysis can take time and effort, but since you will be using these results to drive almost every aspect of your business...it's worth it.

In coaching top advisors I regularly use certain tests to help uncover what makes the advisor tick. Two of the most powerful tests I use are the Kolbe Index and the Financial DNA Path Profiles. These programs are designed to measure your natural instinctive energy — which may be the most critical driver in your life. They are deceptively simple tests that are extremely robust in their impact.

Up until recently, instincts were something we all knew about but couldn't measure. So they were useless from a business perspective because we couldn't quantify them. Kolbe opened the door to instinctive natural strengths and then Financial DNA took it a step further with a focus on the behavioral drivers behind money and investing. The results are extremely valuable. To understand this you need to know about...

## *The three-part mind*

As human beings, we have three basic components that make up the big picture of who we are psychologically:

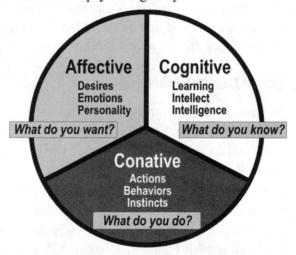

The **Cognitive** Mind deals with intelligence, knowledge and learned ability. The cognitive mind answers the question, *"What do you know?"* We typically quantify learned abilities by using standardized tests such as IQ tests, SATs, Series 7 exam, and the like.

The **Affective** Mind covers desires, emotions, personality and values. It deals the basic question, *"What do you want?"* What are your likes and dislikes? What do you wish for? What do you think is important? What do you prefer? There are several personality-type tests you can take, such as the popular Myers-Briggs.

The **Conative** Mind deals with actions, behaviors and instincts. It answers the question, *"What do you do?"* When faced with a task, a challenge or job to accomplish...how do you proceed? What specific actions do you tend to take?

The cognitive and affective minds are fluid and ever shifting. Learned abilities obviously change every day. Values, preferences and personality can also shift over time. You probably feel differently about certain issues today than you did ten or twenty years ago. And you will twenty years from now. This is totally normal.

Instincts, however, do not change much if at all over your entire life. They are hard-wired inside us and they are very powerful engines that drive our daily actions. They are also unconscious operators. They work when we are under stress, a time crunch, or in new or unfamiliar situations. They are like a hidden computer program that leaps into action when we are in uncharted waters. It is very useful to know what they are and how they control many of the decisions we make and behaviors we manifest.

The first test that I suggest you take is the Kolbe A Index. You will find this at www.kolbe.com. It will take you about twenty minutes and costs about $50. You will get your results right there on-line with a detailed explanation of what everything means from Kolbe.

When I took my Kolbe on the very first day of Strategic Coach, it was like a revelation — like someone had removed a dark shroud from in front of my eyes and said, *"Now do you understand...you idiot?"*

Thousands of decisions I made and actions I took throughout my life rushed screaming into sharp focus. Events from childhood, high school, college, and throughout my professional career were now recast in a new light that formed a much deeper understanding of who I was and am. My only regret was that I didn't take this damn test thirty years ago!

After that, I had to learn more so I went to Arizona and studied with Kathy Kolbe herself to become a certified Kolbe consultant. Armed with that level of understanding...I have incorporated Kolbe analysis into nearly all my training and coaching programs. I try to translate the Kolbe results for reps into specific applications for their business across the spectrum of marketing strategies, client service models, team-building, daily activities, target client types, and stress reduction. I've done this now for years and it's an extremely valuable service.

The second test is the Financial DNA Analysis. This takes a deeper look at your instincts and behaviors surrounding financial issues. It is a fantastic tool for advisors to use with clients. In fact, I think eventually our industry will mandate that some form of this analysis should be part of every advisor's discovery process with the client.

The answers in DNA will tell you specifically what's driving people's attitudes and behaviors about their money. It's almost an unfair advantage. You will be armed with so much useful information that your ability to be understood by the client and to ultimately help them achieve their goals is easily doubled! You do not want to be competing against advisors who are using this tool with their clients. You can reach this test at www.financialdna.net.

Kolbe or Financial DNA alone will tell you a tremendous amount about yourself. You don't need a consultation with anyone to benefit from their analysis. But as a critical next step, I recommend you take your Kolbe and Financial DNA scores and discuss them with someone who has an understanding of both programs and who knows the financial advisory business...like me.

In effect, these tests will get you to the five yard line and I will punch you over the goal toward incorporating this new and powerful understanding of yourself into your practice. This coaching isn't a free service (except for IXIS clients), so don't get too happy yet. If you want more information go to my website at www.frankmaselli.com.

## *What does this have to do with branding?*

Everything!

Let me use my own Kolbe scores as a simple example. In Kolbe language, I'm a 3-3-10-3. That's a maximum initiating Quick Start and a resistant or preventing Fact Finder, Follow Through, and Implementer. (You will understand what these all mean when you take the test.)

If I were to brand myself by claiming that I did thorough financial analysis for clients and dug through mounds of data to uncover the best investment strategies for their financial plan...it would be a total lie! I could never sustain such a branding message by my actions.

Being an initiating Quick Start means I am an innovator, a risk taker, an ad libber, a "ready, fire, aim" sort of person who is more interested in taking action and adjusting on the fly than in careful pre-decision analysis. This frequently drives my wife insane! I will start a hundred projects and finish two. I have a dozen half-read books on my nightstand. On a three-week vacation to Europe, my wife is packed months in advance with all her outfits planned and coordinated for weather and time of day. Me...I am throwing random clothes into a suitcase as the car is pulling into the driveway to take us to the airport.

From a business perspective, there is no way I can base my brand identity on careful, thorough financial analysis. I am much more at home telling stories and painting big pictures of the strategy. Leave the details of managing the money to someone else, preferably a team of smart folks who care about crap like alpha, beta and semi-standard deviations.

If I somehow tried to build that kind of precision business it would cause me tremendous stress, tension and anxiety. Eventually the daily effort required to fight my natural instincts would crush me mentally and emotionally and I would quit or shut down.

My branding message to clients will be that I am going to bring them ideas and strategies they are not likely to get from other advisors (innovator). That I will explain to them clearly the big picture of what, how and why they are doing what I tell them (communicator). I am not going to manage the money myself, but instead I will bring them a team of the best minds on Wall Street to handle their portfolio. I am the quarterback, the CFO, the captain of the ship guiding the overall direction on their behalf.

That pitch may resonate with the client and it may not...but it *is* what I'm actually going to do and do very well. So it would make sense to build my branding message on that set of skills.

Also, from a marketing standpoint, I am not likely to attract clients because of my ability to outperform the indexes. I'm a lot more likely to create an event-based marketing strategy that takes advantage of my natural communication instincts. I need to do lots of big seminars and huge thematic campaigns. Those are not work to me...they're fun!

Oh, that's the other part of instincts, by the way. When you tap into them, your business becomes a giant E-ticket ride to success. You are enjoying things more and having fun every day. Work goes away — in many cases, you don't even feel like you're working at all. You actually experience a sense of weightlessness and power that athletes have described as "being in the zone." It's wonderful when that happens to you...and it can, with some detailed self-awareness.

So my recommendation is to learn as much as you can about yourself before you start to brand a damn thing. There is a metric ton of information locked up inside your head waiting to be discovered. The first step is to dig deep within yourself to uncover the central themes and energies that will drive your actions. They will form the best, most powerful, compelling, and accurate definition of you.

The next step is to...

## Look outside

What do others think about you? Well let's find out. Why not do a client satisfaction survey and ask a few questions? The answers you get back may not only surprise you but might point you in a direction better aligned with your clients' needs.

Many firms do giant surveys of hundreds of thousands of clients, but those measure many items that are beyond your direct control. The idea with a personal survey is to appear *not* as a part of a giant, impersonal organization, but a small team of dedicated professionals devoted to the client.

There are many ways to structure a client survey. Here's one way that works for me and is easy for the client to complete. It starts with a simple letter:

*Dear Client,*

*All of us at the Maselli Group at First Hungarian deeply appreciate that you've chosen us to be your financial advisors. We are on a constant mission to improve the quality of our service to you.*

*To assist us in this process, we ask you to complete this brief satisfaction survey. Your answers will help us to identify those areas where we are successfully meeting your needs and those that may require some improvement. Please do not hesitate to be as open as possible. We value the relationship we've built with you and a cornerstone of that bond is communication.*

*The survey should take you no more than ten minutes to complete but the results will be tremendously valuable toward strengthening our relationship.*

*Thanks again for your continued trust. We look forward to working with you for many years to come.*

*Sincerely,*

*Frank Maselli*

You can build the survey in a variety of ways, but these are the five main subjects I would try to assess:

- **Accessibility:** Are you able to reach us? Are we there when you need us?

- **Empathy:** Do you feel we really take the time to understand you, your needs, dreams, hopes, etc.?

- **Clarity:** Do you understand us and what's going on with your money? Have we explained it in terms that make complete sense to you?

- **Impact:** Do you feel that we are making positive progress toward your most important goals?

- **Proactivity:** Are we thinking ahead or merely reacting to conditions?

- **Improvements:** What can we do to serve you better?

I might add a fill-in-the-blank question to inject the branding concept into my survey: *"If you were telling your best friend or business partner about The Maselli Group...what would you say about us?"*

That's all...nothing too heavy or detailed. These are busy folks and they are not going to spend an hour filling in your survey. All you're looking for is some honest feedback to help you help them. Try it and you will enjoy the results.

## Who else touches your clients?

Everyone who personally interacts with the client plays a role in defining who *you* are. It all counts: even the smallest things that may not mean much individually add up in the mind of the client to create or reinforce (or contradict) an idea about you. They need to be examined and controlled. Ultimately each touch is like a single tile in a giant mosaic that tells "The Story of You." It's that story that leads to referrals.

This idea messaging starts with the office receptionist and continues through every layer of the organization that is likely to touch a client. All client touch points should be regularly tested for quality as well. The lesson I learned in the Army was to *"inspect what you expect."* So as a manager, I would often call my office from a pay phone just to see how my receptionist handled incoming calls. I would also call my top rep's individual phones to see how their assistants performed. You may want to try that or have a friend call in and ask for you. It might surprise you to learn the truth.

When clients or prospects called into my office I wanted them to feel that they had entered an exclusive, upscale boutique. The phone would be answered in a professional and courteous manner and consistently within two rings. The operator would never place someone on pre-emptive hold without first finding out what they needed. If a call was forwarded to a rep's extension, the operator would come back on and handle it again if there was no answer in three rings. This is a people business so all call handling was designed around a personal touch. Clients were being led by a human being to another human being.

If you walked in for an appointment, the receptionist made you feel at home. If she knew you would be waiting for more than a minute, she would offer you a cup of coffee or a soft drink. There was a comfortable sitting area with upscale magazines and books.

Sounds like a lot to worry about. It is...and that's just the receptionist's job! Today you're lucky if your office even *has* a receptionist...but you get the idea. So be sure those touch points are crisp and professional.

## Narrow it down

To be effective, branding experts generally recommend that your message needs to be tightly focused on a small number of concepts. Some even say pick one idea and stick to that to the exclusion of all others.

You will see entire companies attach themselves to a single idea and drive home that message until it's totally implanted in the consumer. A classic example is FedEx that had the great ad phrase, *"FedEx...when it absolutely, positively has to be there...overnight!"* The key word they wanted to own was "overnight" and they eventually captured the vast bulk of the express shipping business.

Being verbose, I rebel at the one word idea. How can a single word describe everything I do for my clients? It obviously can't, but it doesn't need to. Branding is not about communicating *all* your value in a single message. It just needs to set an anchor — an idea that captures the client's attention and distinguishes you from your competition in a simple, repeatable way.

Being repeatable is crucial. Remember your branding message is transmitted to clients for re-transmission to potential referrals. The referral takes place when they are able to tell your story effectively and compellingly to others. If you make it too complex, they won't be able to pass it on. They will never ask for clarity and your brand will die with them in a sea of confusion along with those referrals.

I've met many financial advisors who tell the most elaborate and convoluted stories about themselves. I wonder if they seriously think their clients are able to remember and repeat that story — or if they even care. If you absolutely must have an elaborate story, then so be it, but save it for the marketing brochure. Clients will remember and use only two or three sentences about you, if that much. So create a "Cliffs Notes" version of the grand epic that is you.

A very simple way to think of this process is to imagine your client is talking to their friend. How would they complete this sentence?

# You need to call my advisor because...

- She put together a fantastic financial plan for us.

- He takes the time to really listen to me.

- She really takes great care of us.

- He is always there when I call.

- She has the greatest ideas.

- He kept us totally out of the Tech Wreck back in 2000.

- She took great care of our company's 401(k) plan.

- He does the most amazing seminars you've ever seen.

- She's brilliant and knows how to navigate these markets.

- He uses some very creative and advanced strategies.

- She never follows the crowd.

- He makes everything extremely easy to understand.

- She's an expert on _____.

- He is always quoted in magazines and on the radio.

- She wrote this great book on _____.

- He really knows his stuff.

- She's a senior vice president with some clout.

- He writes articles for the local paper.

- She used to be the branch manager.

- He works with the Gates Foundation.

- She has amazing money managers I've never seen before.

    You can keep going with this list. The magic referral moment will often come down to a one or two sentence conversation. What you are trying to do is manage and direct that moment from a distance. Branding is your referral remote control.

## *A principles-based practice*

I found that for me, a single branding idea was too hard to do. So I decided to try a set of ideas instead. I call these the core principles of my practice. These are the rules that govern all my daily thoughts and activities. They form the base of my professional pyramid. Let me share them with you as an example of what you can do yourself.

- Help advisors succeed — they are why we're here.

- Understand people first — everything else is second.

- We are in the yes business — find ways to get it done.

- Be the best and always work to get better.

- Think big, be bold, and live with passion.

These principles are simple and easy to understand. They act as both a driver and a filter for all my activities and decisions. Before I do anything, I ask myself if it resonates with my core principles. If it does…I do it. If not, I discard it or farm it out.

With only slight modifications, these might work just as well for you in a client advisory practice. Keep it short and simple. I worked hard at trimming down the words to a manageable and memorable few. By contrast, I've seen some advisors with these lengthy mission statements. I appreciate the effort, but who the hell is reading all that? Bullets are better than huge paragraphs. Of course that's a Quick Start speaking.

Also, I would resist the urge to base these business principles too heavily on investment concepts. *"We are core value investors!"* Oh really? What if I need something else…you're not going to help me? There are certainly some fundamental investment principles that make sense, but we are talking about a bigger issue here — your total practice image. For that picture, paint with dynamic colors and inspiring visions. Details dull the view. This is not about managing money…it's about motivating and reaching people on a deep and memorable level.

Once you have your core principles, I would get them engraved on a plaque and put them on my wall. I would print them on all my stationery and set them to pop up on my computer as a screen saver. I would display them on my website and talk about them in my newsletters. They are going to be important to your branding message so I would try to make them as visible as possible to everyone on my team as well as clients and prospects and visitors.

Clients may not quote your principles to their friends when referring you, but the fact that you *have* a set of principles in the first place is going to make you appear more professional and worthy of referrals.

You now have a story, you have taken a position. You are a potent force for good with a powerful self-belief that is compelling to top clients and centers of influence. Your branding image becomes one of professionalism, energy, and success. This is the feeling that will get transmitted during the referral conversation.

---------------------

## NOTE:

For a detailed discussion of how to craft a simple yet powerful branding message, you want to read the wonderful book by Mark Magnacca called *The Product Is You*. Mark will help you master this critical concept in a very useful and enjoyable way!

Go to www.insightdevelopment.com for more information today.

*Referral Strategy #8*

# Use The New Specialty Referral

## Concept overview:

- Your long-term clients may be the perfect source of potential referrals. But if you've never asked them for referrals before...you are changing the implied rules of the relationship game as you've both played it for many years.

- They might misinterpret your sudden request as a sign of business weakness.

- The new specialty referral lets you go back to your best clients for referrals without looking like you just blew up your business.

- It also sends the right emotional messages about your success and development as a professional.

This strategy is designed primarily for more seasoned advisors who have had some clients for several years, but it can be used by anyone. If you are an experienced advisor and you have not been regularly asking for referrals from your top clients, you run an extra risk when you do so.

The risk is that the client may think your business has taken a turn for the worse. Something may have gone wrong! And that's not the right message to send...not only because it's not true, but also because it can have a significant negative impact on the relationship. And the worst part is that you may never know it's happening.

Many years ago, I started on a mini-referral campaign *without* this approach and it bit me on the butt. I actually had a good client say to me after I asked him for some names, *"What happened Frank, did you blow up your book?"*

He was joking...or was he? I could tell there was a note of concern in there somewhere. How he knew the phrase *"blow up your book"* should have made me wonder since it's an industry insider kind of term, but he was right...that is exactly how it must have looked to him.

To go from *never* asking to *suddenly* asking is often so uncomfortable a move that many seasoned professional advisors will not take the risk with their most trusted clients...even though those are potentially the best sources of top referrals.

Every client/advisor relationship has a certain set of terms, conditions, and expected behaviors for both parties. To violate those on either side is to shake things up too violently and could cause longer-term issues. The client may begin to view you and your recommendations in a new weaker light.

By adding the new specialty into the referral mix, you avoid any of those issues and, simultaneously, you send exciting positive messages of growth and success. Here's how to do it:

## How to choose a specialty

First it has to be interesting to you personally. Forcing yourself to specialize in something that holds no emotional appeal to you, even though it might be important to the clients, is going to be a rough road for you. Your messaging will not carry the powerful enthusiasm needed to get clients interested in using you to do this thing.

Second I would choose an area that has less competition. If your top clients are likely to hear the same "specialty" story from several advisors in town, it invalidates the concept.

Finally, I would select something that can add real value to the client's world. Anyone can call themselves a "retirement expert," but how many advisors are "Certified Lifestyle Planners." These professionals are trained to help folks handle the hundred other decisions and situations that come with retirement beyond the relatively simple world of money and investing. I view this as an extreme value-added service you can provide top clients that truly makes you special.

## What can I specialize in?

I am not talking about getting a CFP or a CIMA, although that would be nice. Basically all I mean is a certain degree of expertise in a specific area. In this business, that could take you literally a few days of study and research.

The new specialty can be any one of a vast list of items from traditional investment topics to more esoteric, non-financial areas. Here is a list of some potential areas in which you might want to specialize:

- Business lending

- Non-qualified deferred compensation

- Insurance and estate planning

- Alternative minimum tax issues

- Lifestyle planning

- 401(k) plans

- Mortgages

- Real estate investing

- International bonds

- Options

- Commodities

- Hedge funds

- Managed money

Your new specialty can be a product or service or it can also be a theme...which may be even better because it may encompass multiple products. An example of a powerful theme might be:

**International investing** — Placing a portion of investor assets overseas makes tremendous sense from several perspectives. First, you open up the portfolio to a vast world of potential investment ideas many of which are growing a lot faster than companies here at home. Second is diversification. Although correlations on foreign markets versus the U.S. market shrink periodically, they still provide significant risk reduction to a totally US-based portfolio.

**Diversify your fixed-income** — Many fixed-income investors have the bulk of their bond portfolios in domestic Treasuries or agency securities. This can be good and bad. Certainly a government backing (or moral obligation) carries very low risk of default, but in a rising rate environment, triple-A rated paper has no place to go but down. This may be the time to own foreign bonds, high yields, REITs, MLPs, convertibles, and preferred stocks. It's also a great time to explore bond – alternatives, such as dividends from common stocks as an income generator.

**Absolute return strategies** — It may make sense for some clients to have a piece of their portfolio in the hands of money managers who pursue a more absolute return approach. As they say, *"You can't eat relative return."* An absolute return portfolio may use a wide variety of instruments and tactics in an attempt to deliver positive performance in almost any kind of market or economic environment. They are relatively unconstrained and may make big sector bets, go short, or hedge with options and derivatives. This is not for everyone, but used wisely, it can be a productive part of the client's portfolio.

**Retirement income strategies** — Many investors will be making the transition from the accumulation phase of their retirement plan to the distribution phase over the next several years. Their needs are more complex than they might think and a pure bond portfolio won't do the trick. How can you help them generate the kind of income they need while still growing their principal? Which asset classes and disciplines blend well together to create this kind of diversified distribution portfolio? How can you use strategies like covered call and immunized bonds to enhance income and maintain growth?

**Core and satellite portfolios** — The old buy and hold strategies of the past may not be as productive in the future. One new structure is the core and alpha satellite strategy. Here you place the core 75% of the portfolio with a diversified, rebalanced set of managers and you take the remaining 25% and seek alpha from non-traditional, low-correlation asset classes or disciplines.

**Lifestyle planning** — This is the next generation of a relationship with top clients. Lifestyle planning involves helping a client in ways that go beyond money and investing. It digs into subjects like the client's life goals for post-retirement years; healthcare planning; and other meaningful long-term goals.

## Not overnight

Obviously you cannot become a true expert in any area overnight. But initially, that may not even be your goal. You need to know only enough to carry on an intelligent conversation and ask good, probing questions. Then you need to know who to go to for real answers. With experience over time, the skill develops, and sooner than you think, you'll be writing books on the subject.

Chances are that most "specialties" you select can be developed in little more than a week or two of focused reading and conversations with experts right in your own firm or business community. The Internet can deliver more information to your desktop than you can even imagine.

But worst case let's say it takes you a month of research to understand a topic of specialization that could open you up to new clients. Is your business worth one month of intense study? I'm thinking it is. And once you have the knowledge it's yours forever…so pick something you enjoy and get started today. Ironically, one of the best sources of information on a particular subject might even be a client.

So now you have a specialty…what next?

## The new specialty conversation

Once you have your "new specialty" in place, you're ready to talk with the client.

**– Advisor**

*"Hi Bob, It's Jim over at First Hungarian...how are you?"*

**– Client**

*"Great Jim, nice to hear from you...what's up?"*

**– Advisor**

*"A whole bunch actually. I wanted to chat with you about something that my team and I have been working on for some time now. It's a new specialty that we've developed in an area of investing that I think will help you a lot."*

**– Client**

*"Very interesting...tell me more."*

**– Advisor**

*"Well...(and you briefly tell the story of your new specialty)"*

**– Client**

*"That's very interesting, Jim. It sounds like it might make a lot of sense for me."*

**– Advisor**

*"I thought so too. In fact...I think a lot of folks in your position might be very interested in this as well. Let me run something by you Bob. Your firm holds their quarterly partners' meeting in January...is that right."*

**– Client**

*"Yes...the 15$^{th}$ through the 20$^{th}$ in Boca."*

**– Advisor**

*"I would like to come down and do a fifteen-minute overview of this idea to the group. I am very excited about this and have a great presentation that will explain the whole thing in very simple language. I'm sure that agenda is pretty busy so that's why I'm*

*calling you now. This is just one of those ideas that people need to hear about and frankly, very few of my colleagues even understand how this works. It's a bit complex and takes time to master. We decided over a year ago that we were going to become experts in this and we were way ahead of the curve."*

### – Client

*"Well, I will have to bounce that off Gail. She is the managing partner and it would be her call to get you on the agenda. But I will let you know."*

### – Advisor

*"That sounds great. If you like...the three of us can go to dinner next week. I can show her what we would talk about in Boca. This is not a sales pitch...she may want to know that. But I think your partners would be very interested in at least learning more...and I could be a good resource for the firm if anyone wants more information."*

In this case you're asking Jim to set up a meeting with Gail, the boss. If your client is NOT the ultimate decision maker for what you're asking, then you should always try to get in front of that person directly. Your client is not an expert in the idea and may not know how best to explain it to their boss.

You also may not be fully aware of the relationship your client has *to* the boss. Human nature being what it is, your client may have overstated the importance of their position in the firm and you could have the wrong advocate driving the process. Far better to ask for a simple introduction than for them to take on your cause within the group you're targeting.

Conversely, if you do have the right person and the right idea, you may not need to do anything. They may run with the ball entirely on your behalf and you're all set. You've generated a number of potential referrals while looking very smart and successful in the eyes of your existing client. And in the process, you may have made them look good to the people they care about, which can't be anything but great!

Is this a little bold? Perhaps, but you're sending an exciting, positive message to the client here. You're saying you are growing, learning, and expanding the spectrum of services you offer clients. These are all very good things.

With the New Specialty Referral, you never have to look weak or desperate in the client's eyes. Quite the opposite…business is booming!

By the way…if a client ever asks, there is only one answer to the question, **"How's business?"**

"Business is fantastic!" And if you don't want to lie just say, "Amazing! You have no idea. It's incredible. Un-freaking-believable!"

*Referral Strategy #9*

# Use The Event Referral

## Concept overview:

- HNW clients love events and they are willing to bring their friends and colleagues if you give them something exciting and entertaining to attend.

- The event referral is low risk for the client because the referral gets to make the decision about you on their own. The client doesn't need to sell you...just the event.

- These can be tremendously fun to do and can form the cornerstone of your marketing efforts.

- Events are useful for getting referrals from the children of your older, wealthier clients. ("The Paris Hilton Syndrome")

There are hundreds of potential events you can use to generate referrals from top clients.

You're limited only by your creativity and budget. These include everything from seminars to golf outings to cooking classes to spa days to art gallery openings to wealth management "boot camps" for trust fund babies. I couldn't even list the things available to you. Almost any type of event where people gather can become a referral opportunity, so don't get wrapped up in the specific type of event just yet.

Let's first look deeper into the general nature of these events and give you the actual tools you need to design your own. Here are the broad characteristics an ideal referral event would possess.

## *Upscale*

Choose an activity and location that fit the types of clients you're inviting — something to which they would be proud to bring their friends and colleagues. That implies a nice location and appropriate preparation work. This might cost some money. I know one rep who spends on average more than $100,000 per year on client events like these. He does an annual dinner at a fancy hotel in Beverly Hills and invites clients and their friends for an evening of dining and dancing. Very nice…but it's like doing a wedding every year! In fact, some of his clients have taken to calling it "the wedding." Even he has fun with this, asking, *"Are you coming to the wedding?"*

When he addresses the group, he talks about things like family and a bond and how the relationship between an advisor and client is a lot like a marriage of sorts. Naturally, there is tremendous fodder for humor, this being Hollywood and all. But the overarching message is one of family and social intimacy. These themes in contrast to a numbers-based business work wonders and position him as very different from his competition.

As for the hundred grand…he's not even at the top of the list for spending. I know advisors who spend a lot more on their clients and referral events. How about hunting and fishing treks to Kenya, New Zealand and Alaska? How about three-day retreats to Canyon Ranch with six couples and their kids?

When it comes to growing your business…what would you spend to do it right? That depends a lot on how much you *have* to spend and on whom you're going after. The whales these advisors are vying for aren't coming to the Holiday Inn to learn how to "Save for Retirement." And they're not going bowling (although bowling is rumored to be making a comeback, I'm told).

For most of us…the correct style and scale of the event comes down to more mundane decisions. Should you hold it at a country club, a local restaurant or a hotel? How many people should you invite and what should you serve as refreshments?

How much you spend is a function of your overall marketing budget, but you should be putting roughly 10% of the gross back into the business. So if you're a million-dollar producer, to spend $100,000 on your business isn't too much. Given all the other things you might need (like a fully paid assistant), that might leave you with $35,000 to $45,000 per year to spend on event marketing.

You can do some nice stuff for that kind of money. OK, Canyon Ranch may not work, but it's something to aspire to. Wouldn't you love to have the kind of business where spending $3 million to $5 million on it would be justifiable? Maybe…maybe not. But it is happening out there among a small group of top advisors.

*How realistic is that 10% number? Not very! Let's say that an advisor grossing $1 million nets maybe $450,000 pretax at a major firm. That's what…$300,000 after tax? And I'm saying put $100,000 back into the business! How crazy is that?*

*Your business should be the best investment you can make with your money. If not…there's something wrong with your model. Also…too many of us have built our lifestyles on the best trailing 12 of 60 level. That's too high off the hog. Start scaling back and learn to live like half the producer you are. That will keep you liquid enough to take advantage of leverage opportunities to drive your business along a much steeper growth curve.*

My general advice is don't skimp out, but don't go insane either. There is a "shrimp factor" involved here. ***"The bigger the shrimp…the worse the deal"*** was the way we used to judge investment banking launches back in the day. Go too high falutin' for your target audience and you may have people wondering about your fees. Go too low and they may wonder about your success. So it's a balancing act that you will base on the clients you're inviting and the type of messages you want to send.

If you're stuck, ask one of the clients you plan to invite for their opinion. You will generally get a good feel from them as to what's appropriate or too over the top.

## *Valuable*

The event should impart real knowledge (without a sales pitch) that top people could use. It would be intellectually stimulating and rewarding. Time is the HNW client's (and their referral's) most precious commodity, hence they are always weighing its alternative uses. The basic question they ask themselves is, *"Should I do one of the hundred things I love and need to do or do I go to your event?"*

Recognizing that time is more valuable than money is one of the most critical things you can do when working with HNW clients. This reality transcends referrals. Everything you do in your business should be geared around this fundamental understanding. Make my life easier and save me time — both real clock time and mental time — and we're going to have a great relationship.

If your event involves teaching, like a seminar or symposium for example, make sure what you're teaching them is geared toward their world and is giving them information and wisdom they are not getting anywhere else. That means your content — and the way you market it — must be appropriate. Bill it as "advanced" and add some spin that would appeal to HNW clients.

As many of you know, I love seminars. I used to do several different kinds of seminars with topics that included everything from reducing taxes to saving for retirement to international investing. I found that my seminar results were almost always better when I included a section in my talk called **"What Your Broker Doesn't Want You To Know!"**

This was the part of the seminar when I talked mainly about fees, commissions and risks...the three critical areas of client concern that most advisors shied away from or tried to downplay.

By including a section like this, I got credit for being on the client's side. There was an implied irreverence and criticism of the rest of the industry and it put me in a position to stand out from the crowd.

Was I discussing anything secret or unknown? Not really, but I made it *feel* that way and the audiences loved it. Invariably, it was the part that drew the most active response from the audience and the one they remembered most. Do this well and they will both believe and remember you a lot better.

# *Fun*

People of all demographics want to have fun. There should be some entertainment content associated with an event. Now, education can be entertaining so there is a bit of overlap here. But this might also include a sporting event of some kind or some other spectator event.

Obviously anything that's enjoyable to watch could be an enjoyable event, but you should examine the dynamic of the event itself. Some things, like theater, are not my favorite because they allow for very limited interaction.

Sports are better, but even there, some sports are terrible for interaction. Hockey, basketball, soccer, lacrosse, volleyball...all of these are what could be called "constant motion" sports. There's very little time for conversation. Much better to attend a baseball game, football game, or pro golf tourney, where there's plenty of time to relax between stuff happening on the field.

As fun as *watching* something may be...participation is ten times better! Get people doing something enjoyable and you will bond with them for a long time. Anything that can be watched can be done. This is true for almost all professional sports, hobbies and performance-type events. So instead of going to a game...play a game!

You're thinking, *"I can't play football with my clients!"* OK...maybe that's an extreme example. But in general, HNW clients today are fitter and more capable than they were a few generations ago. Getting people up and out even for a little while under supervised conditions is a memorable blast.

I'm not the most in-shape guy anymore, and when I was told that, as part of our national meeting, my entire department was going to play paintball...I was more than a bit skeptical. But I have to say that it was fantastic! We were all in alien territory learning something new together. It was competitive, which many HNW clients enjoy. It was exciting to do and fun to watch, even after I got shot and eliminated, so there was constant participation and energy flow. And the buzz that stayed with the group for days afterwards was thrilling.

So why not sponsor that kind of thing for your clients? Too wild for such a diverse group? Then maybe you pick one client and do the event for their company managers. Or pick two CEO clients and pit their companies against each other in a friendly war. Then when you get there...switch CEOs. This is a great way to shake things up and to bond to the number-two person in the company, who becomes the immediate de facto leader of the group. Or pick one client and have him invite another department from within his own company. The dynamics are endless and all fun to experience.

The point is that referral events don't have to be the typical seminar or dinner meeting. You have many choices so open up to other ideas.

## *Exciting*

Adding to the fun theme, HNW folks are eager for bold, new experiences...so give them some, under controlled conditions of course. I'm not talking about climbing Mount Ranier, but maybe deep sea fishing or playing a new golf course they haven't been to can be exciting. Maybe you could host a corporate Outward Bound event for your top client's company.

What would be the benefit of an event like this to you? Well, you're not just an investment professional, you're the client's partner. You're deeply involved in and concerned with their success and their company's success. An event like Outward Bound or any of a dozen other corporate team-building programs helps *them*...not you. It's about putting their needs first...which may be the greatest referral-generating philosophy anyone can have.

## *Unique*

Your event should have a certain cache to it. It should be something that is a bit uncommon and special...just like the people you're inviting. Take me someplace I haven't been before. Or get me behind the scenes someplace that only a few folks get to visit.

A rep I know held a cocktail party backstage at Radio City Music Hall in New York. There's a special room in which the owners used to have private parties. You walk through it on the Radio City tour but she rented it out and had a fantastic seminar there. Very classy and fun.

Find a venue in your community that is a little off the beaten path. Think differently and more boldly. Be creative. Now I know that in this world of compliance hell, creativity is a foul word to some, but there is no regulation governing where you can hold an event. I've seen everything from a Washington State winery to the aircraft carrier Intrepid in Manhattan…to dare I say it…the Playboy Mansion. Personally I wouldn't want Elliott Spitzer to see that expense report, so I'm staying closer to the mainstream…but have some fun. This business used to be fun and it can be again.

It's not just location; your content can be unique as well. I know one great wholesaler who is helping his reps do seminars that include experts on identity theft from the FBI. He developed a relationship with the local FBI office and has been helping advisors pack the house with this increasingly timely topic.

## Involve multi-levels of family

Family is one of the biggest, if not *the* biggest concern people have and the types of events you create will depend on the various audiences you're trying to reach.

### From soccer clinics to financial boot camps

Clients with young children want to spend quality time with them. Coming to your event ranks well below that desire, but by giving them a chance to do both, you may solve that problem.

For example, hold a Saturday soccer clinic for the kids of your top clients and their friends. Hire the soccer coach from the local college and maybe a few players as well. These clients are very interested in their kids and grandkids and sports may be a big part of the child's life. Depending on the age and interests of your clients' children, this could be a homerun.

While the kids are kicking the ball around…you're hosting a nice breakfast event in a tent adjacent to the field. Have a photographer there to take action shots of the kids. Frame and send them to your guests as a nice follow-up gift.

This works with almost any sport and the homework you do on the client will tell you what their kids are playing. You might actually uncover links to potential prospects through the children!

Not into sports? How about an acting clinic, a computer class, a nature day, a hayride, or a free day at the aquarium or the zoo? Take it from me, there is almost nothing parents won't do to have some kind of enjoyable learning excursion with their young kids. Tap into that vein and you're going to reach a lot of great potential clients for not very much money.

Clients with older children have different concerns. For example, many wealthy parents are desperate for ideas that will help prevent their kids from turning out like rich, spoiled brats. Some call this the *Paris Hilton Syndrome*. Hey...I have two young daughters myself! I'm not busting my butt every day to see them show up on the cover of the *Girls Gone Wild* DVD. How can values be passed along with money? How can kids be prepared to handle the responsibility that comes with wealth?

Many private banks today are running financial "boot camps" for their wealthy clients and their older children. As the Baby Boomers mature, this wealth transfer issue is going to be a massive concern. You may want to consider a program like that. Some of these programs can be fairly elaborate and held in exotic locales that draw the attention of the jet set. But more important is the content itself. I believe most HNW families would say, *"Save the glitz. We can do that ourselves. Just give us the value and the content."*

## Give back

HNW clients are generally very interested in giving back to their community. An event that is attached in some way to a charity or a cause like this would be a good draw.

Here again, the work you've done in uncovering their interests pays off. You can host a golf tournament to support the client's charity. This also positions you as a partner and ally in a way that transcends money. I would suggest you only do it if you really believe in the cause yourself. You want to bring a real enthusiasm for the effort that outshines any possible critique of your motive.

When you're doing your client research, pay particular attention to those causes to which the client devotes time rather than money. Money may be gold...but each minute of my day is a diamond!

Check out the local calendars in the communities in which your clients live. In fact, I'd make it a point to get and read the local papers for my top twenty clients' hometowns. Sounds like a lot of work, right?

Well, remember, your job is people…not investing. Find out what's going on around them and what they might be participating in that you can help with.

## *Displays you well*

Certain types of referral events should have a focus on you to some degree. I like to do events where I can display some of my skills. For example, at every event I do, I speak to the audience for at least a few minutes. That's arguably my number-one skill and I want my prospective clients to see me in action.

Obviously, this skill would be the centerpiece at an event like a seminar, symposium, client dinner, and the like. But almost anything you might do would give you a chance to bring folks together and get their attention for a few minutes. In truth, I will find a way to talk to the group no matter what the event may be. It's that important to my success.

Similarly, I would probably avoid events where my lack of skill was highlighted. I can play golf or shoot clays with anyone because I don't take it too seriously and I can occasionally hit amazing shots or score respectably. But I'm not going white water rafting with a group of clients and potential referrals. The first time they see me dive to the middle of the boat cowering and sobbing like a little girl will damage my professional credibility.

People make decisions about you based on a vast number of factors, including how you carry and conduct yourself at an event and how you perform various tasks. In simple terms, if you're a good golfer, speaker, fisherman, shooter, tennis player, etc., they extrapolate to some degree that you must be good at other things, including investing and finance.

If you're bad…maybe you're not a total loser but you have a subconscious hill to climb in their minds. Even more superficially, people will judge you on appearance first. So even if you're a lousy golfer, you should dress and look like a good one.

Is this fair or accurate? No…but it's human nature. There is no correlation between my ability to consistently hit a low crossing pair of battues at forty-five yards or drive a ball beyond the fairway bunkers and my ability to manage a multi-million-dollar portfolio. Or is there? Isn't there some part of us that says, "Success breeds success?" I don't have the deep psychological answers. All I know from experience is I'd rather be doing something that makes me look good than bad in the eyes of my clients and prospects.

## Why do event referrals work so well?

Event referrals can become a powerful part of your overall referral strategy if you do them well. They require a commitment of time, energy and resources so they are not for everyone. In general, they are good for a few reasons:

### They position you as a person of influence.

At the basic level, these events are a gathering of successful, HNW people coming together for a common purpose. To be attached to that, to be the *cause* of that, is to position yourself as an important person in their collective world. You look like a mover and shaker...someone capable of making things happen and influencing others. That is all good.

### They get a group dynamic working for you.

There are things that can happen in group settings that cannot happen one –on one. If you have a successful event that people enjoy, they actually enjoy it more in a group than if they experienced it alone. Bringing people together in some venue is a great way to create positive feelings about what you do. But again, it presupposes that you're doing the kind of event that we described.

### They are low risk to the client.

With an event referral, the client doesn't have to sell you to their friend. You get to do that for yourself by doing a great event. If you pull it off, the friend turns to the client and says, *"Hey this guy is great!"* Done...referral locked up! The friend made the choice...they liked you and the client's work is done. Even better, the client actually looks good in their friend's eyes for having invited them to the event and for being associated with someone as dynamic as you.

If you screw up, the client has plausible deniability. They get to disavow you and have very little risk to themselves. The friend says,

*"Wow that was terrible!"* The client agrees, they throw you under the bus, and they're off the hook.

In this way, however, event referrals are higher risk/return processes to you. Be aware that every time you bring people together, you increase your leverage opportunities for both good and bad results. So my advice is to make sure you're wired with aces back to back! Be totally sure of your ability to pull off a great event. Leverage is your greatest business-building ally, but it can turn on you and instead of losing one referral on a bad night...you just lost 50!

## The Unique Ability thing

At the heart of most types of event referrals is you doing what you do best. Letting people see you in this success mode is a great way to bond to them. At The Strategic Coach they call this your "Unique Ability." Let people see you doing this thing and they will be impressed because, by definition, you're impressive at it! At the very least they leave feeling good about some part of you. This Unique Ability concept is so powerful that it's worth the entire tuition at Strategic Coach, even though it's only one of a hundred things they teach you in that amazing program.

After talking about referrals and Unique Ability at a Merrill Lynch branch once, I had a FA tell me, *"Frank, based on what you're saying here...I'm screwed!"*

He went on to say that he loved one thing more than anything else in his life...golf! He loved it so much he was on the golf course every day before the market opened and after the market closed.

Now that's a problem, I thought, but I wanted to learn more because he seemed so passionate about this.

He then said, *"But you don't understand...I'm really good at golf."* At this point the other FAs began to snicker. I wasn't sure why and thought he was just boasting. *"OK...how good are you?"* I asked defiantly.

*"Well I led the U.S. Open for two rounds."*

That's a phrase you don't hear every day. *"What are you talking about...who are you?"* I asked incredulously.

He went on to say that he was a PGA card-carrying professional and had a handicap of –minus two. That means you have to add two strokes to his game to get him up to par! It was killing him that he now had to give up golf because his manager told him to get in and pound the phones to grow his business.

This is not enlightened advice. This guy should never set foot in the branch. And I told him exactly what I would suggest he do.

First get a golf cart built in the shape of the Merrill Lynch bull. I will even tell you the company that can build it for you.  I'm talking a big head with horns on the front and a wagging tail in the rear. Take this golf cart to every country club in a 300-mile radius where you are friends with the local pro. (The FA was a well-known and well-liked celebrity in the local world of golf in his area.) Tell the local pro that you want to set up a playing lesson with the top eight players at the club and that he (the local pro) should participate. Be sure to spend money at the local pro shop…you must let the local guy wet his beak and get a taste of what you're doing here.

Folks…who plays golf at country clubs? Rich people! Potential clients all. This is a fantastic demographic to pursue. But there's one thing missing from this perfect marketing strategy. He needs a team!

He needs a couple of green eye-shade, CFA, CFP types back there in the office to do the things he can't or doesn't like to do. His Unique Ability is not setting up financial plans…it is meeting and bonding to people. And when he is asked on the course, *"What kind of financial advisor can you be if you're out playing golf every day?"* he needs an answer based in conviction.

*"I'm the advisor who will keep you invested for the next 90,000 DOW points. And the best way I can do that is to get your head out of the day-to-day market, get your face away from CNBC, and show you how to enjoy your life. I have a team of folks who do the money stuff and together we are helping wealthy people all over the state."*

Now this works for him for one reason that it would not work for you. He's a MINUS two!  People *want* to play with him.  He can actually teach them something. He's very good! No one is lining up to play with Fat Frankie…the twenty-five! I don't get invited to member guest tournaments. In fact I seldom ever get invited to play a second time anywhere…which bears some reflection I think. He will build a huge referral-based business because he's operating in his deepest passion and people extrapolate success. Plus his main job is to get them in the door and then his teammates can do the financial magic.

Do your Unique Ability every day for as long as you can and build your entire business around it. Success will follow...there's almost no way to stop it. And do yourself another favor and get into Strategic Coach. Stop thinking about it and sign up. I never shill for anything I don't believe in. This is life-changing stuff and you need to experience it. Go to www.strategiccoach.com to learn more.

## *General rules*

There are a few standard referral rules for any type of event.

### Welcome everyone warmly

Whatever the event, the rule of thumb is that within ten seconds of arriving, someone on your team must warmly greet the client and their guest with a big, genuine smile and thank them for coming. Since you can't be all places at once, make sure you have a people who know the clients' names and the names of their guests at the door. The hotel industry has figured out that the greeting is critical to the overall experience of the stay, so they have mastered the art of initial greeting. Take a cue from the Four Seasons and do this as well.

This potentially implies a large, well-trained staff of folks. You may have to hire temps for the event. However you handle it, the worst thing is to have people wandering around feeling unwelcome because you're tied up or too distracted.

What if you don't know the guest's name in advance? Obviously the client should introduce you, but be prepared to take the initiative. I might have a sign-in sheet at the door or if things are busy I might give the guest a little sign-in card they can fill out at their seat and give back to me. Make these a unique color so your assistant can spot them in the room and walk around gathering them when things quiet down a bit.

### Make the client feel special

After they've had a chance to come in and get settled, I will come over again and get into a one- or two-minute mini-conversation. This can be a bit more personal and friendly beyond what a greeting at the door might be.

The referral is watching this interaction like a hawk...so think about the messages you want to convey. Your first attention needs to be on the client. It doesn't matter if they brought Bill Gates to your event and he was standing there with a pen poised over an open checkbook...they are the client and that makes them more important than anyone.

You want to bring the referral into the conversation at some point and you can take a cue from the client. Remember also, you may not know the exact nature of the relationship between a client and their guest. This could be boss-subordinate, subordinate-boss, peer-peer, friend, or any of a hundred other connections. The more you can find out in advance the better, but now is not the time to do a sales pitch. The event must carry its own weight. This is a moment to show how you generally interact with your clients.

Once I am aware of the connection between the client and guest, I will make reference to that link in warmly bringing the guest into the conversation.

"It's pleasure to meet you, Tom. Bob has told me quite a few tall tales about your hunting trips to Borneo."

"Bob has told me some fantastic things are going on over there at Acme Widget. You must be very excited (happy, proud)."

"Bob tells me that you have a wicked short game."

Keep the "I" stuff out of the conversation. Try to focus on the client and the guest. This is not the time for a commercial either. Avoid name dropping and trying to sound too big. There will be time for that later if you must. The goal of this little interaction is to make the client look good in the eyes of their guest in subtle and professional ways. You're trying to suggest that there's an inner circle here and Bob is a member. The guest is getting a glimpse into that circle, but Bob's already in.

Human beings want to belong and feel important. The way you treat Bob will be seen and mildly envied by his guest, thus making him want to get into the inner circle as well. It's all very subliminal and delicate, but it's the way we are hardwired and there's no sense fighting it. Rather, understand it and work with it.

You might even try the Pull Away Conversation. This is where you lead Bob away from his guest for thirty seconds or less to have a private chat about something with him. You laugh, you smile, you talk in low tones just barely audible to the guest. This reinforces the feeling of the inner circle and now he wants in badly!

I might also invite them both to stick around after the talk to meet the guest speaker. If they cannot stay, then I might bring the guest speaker over to meet them now. Again...all under the heading of making the client look good in the guest's eyes.

## No heavy-duty sales pitch

Whatever kind of event you're doing, it should not be covered by an aggressive sales presentation on anything. Even a pure seminar, which would be the event closest to a traditional selling process, needs to be purely educational, upbeat and inspirational.

The product you're selling is you. Not the variable annuity, mutual fund, money manager, or insurance policy. You sell yourself by doing the things we've described not by clouding the content with product.

To do a product sales type event almost guarantees that you're not going to have much success winning over the guests. On top of that, you just exposed your clients to serious fallout for being so intense and pushy. There's no way they will bring other friends to future events.

They are there to have fun, learn some very valuable stuff, and meet you. That's all you need to accomplish. The 200-slide PowerPoints or the six guest portfolio managers who all say the same thing are going to kill them and you in the process.

## *Some rules of business golf*

Golf is a big part of our business and it's worth spending a few minutes on some aspects of the game as it relates to the event referral.

If you're doing a golf event, there are several additional rules that apply. The first concerns timing of the business conversation. You have to pace yourself in a golf event. You're going to be together for quite a bit of time and if you start off on the first tee with a detailed analysis of the managed money universe...you're doomed.

First decide how you're going to mix things up. Let's say you're playing with the client and two guests. Ideally you can play teams for six holes each and partner with each of the other players, including your client. Obviously you want to bond with the guests and this give you a chance to get them in the cart for an hour or more.

Be relaxed and don't push. Let the referral bring up investing first if possible. Use the client's relationship as a catalyst and lead in to the discussion. Get to know the person and display interest in their story before you start talking about yourself and your business

But you do need to talk business...right? Maybe! This is where you have to feel your way around. The ultimate purpose of playing referral golf is to generate business...so there comes a point when you have to assess this possibility. The referral knows why they're there and they know what you do. If they haven't brought up the subject themselves, you may want to. How you do it will depend on the tone of the conversation you've had thus far in the round. But it's always easier to start slow and work up speed. It's much harder to start aggressive and work toward relaxed.

The caveat to this is where you get the feeling that by *not* talking business at all you may actually be sending a better message. I've had people tell me, *"I liked that you never tried to sell me anything on the golf course, Frank. That we could just relax and get to know each other a bit."* So that works too. The bottom line is you have to be sensitive and learn how to read people...which is about ten million times more important and harder than managing the money.

## %$#*@! game

How you conduct yourself on the course is another major issue. It's been said that you really get to know someone when you play golf with them. I couldn't agree more. You see people in a broad range of situations with a wide distribution of emotional states over the course of a five-hour round. Your guests will probably have formed a pretty concrete opinion about you by the eighteenth green and you will have one about them as well.

I'm not going to tell you how to behave on the golf course. As you know, golf can be an extremely frustrating experience at times and I am not a good role model for calm behavior in that setting. The best advice I can give you is to try to relax a bit and enjoy the experience. Remember why you're there. Business golf is not about the score. It's about bonding and letting people see that you can fit into their world.

So don't snap or throw clubs. You will look insane.

Don't drink too much. There's never any professional upside to that.

Try not to curse too much. This is hard for me but try to keep it to a profanity level that is a notch or two below your guest.

Don't play too slow, especially if you're bad. Nothing is more frustrating than watching a really horrid golfer take seven practice swings before each shot knowing that he's only topping the ball twenty yards at a time. You want to scream, "Why bother?"

Don't spend all day looking for lost balls. This isn't a Lewis & Clark journey to the western passage. I carry dozens and will take a drop after thirty seconds. Yes balls are not cheap, but it's the cost of doing business, my friend.

And never cheat!

Wait…a little cheating is part of the game right?

Never! He who cheats in golf will take my money and run off to Bolivia. There's a direct correlation between cheating in golf and the perception of you doing jail time in the mind of the prospect. How can I trust you with my family's future if I can't trust you to play it where it lies?

Even when no one is watching? Especially then! Or when you land in a divot and one of the other players says, *"Oh go ahead and move that ball. It's OK…I'm not looking."* Never! I'd rather take a twelve. And I'm not the golf police. You want to cheat…go ahead. But not me. It's a subliminal line that cannot be crossed and by *not* being crossed gets even stronger and extends favorably into other parts of your world.

At some level, golf is about character. How you handle adversity, disappointment, failure as well as success, exultation, victory. Character counts in our profession. Whatever the name on the door of your office…the ultimate name is yours.

## The tee shot

Let's stay with golf for a minute. Most professionals say, *"You drive for show and putt for dough."* I disagree. To me there is no more important shot in the world of client golf than the drive off the first tee. That followed by every drive for the next seventeen holes.

The drive is the only shot where conditions are optimal and where everyone is looking at you. It is performance under pressure. It is the one shot you can reliably prepare for with consistent practice because you can replicate most of the conditions on any driving range…so it speaks to your discipline and training. When you hit it, you get immediate feedback from your teammates on a great shot or you take immediate ribbing.

If your partners are strangers, you will be immediately judged by this first shot. Expectations will be set. You know what I'm talking about. I've been in groups where the whole character of the interpersonal dynamic hinges on this first shot.

You don't need more pressure on this moment, but I can absolutely guarantee that I lost business in the past because of the first tee. I could feel my confidence slip. I have a slice like an F-22 Raptor making a 9-G missile evading turn! I keep expecting the ball to pop flares as it banks hard right. It's tricky to bring up the subject of the prospect's portfolio after slicing two into the water.

Step into the box and let one fly down the middle for about 250 yards and you're on your way to millions in net new assets. Personally, I think putts should count only half a stroke. They don't even feel like part of the same game. Yes they are pressure moments too, especially with money on the line, so I don't dismiss them entirely as a measure of skill. But to claim that a one-foot tap-in should count as much as a 300-yard drive is ludicrous.

Maybe I'm missing something. I'm sorry, but this is not the PGA Tour…this is *client* golf. Putting is something little kids do through windmills and big clown heads. Anything close is a "gimme" anyway. A perfect drive feels more like high-explosive artillery — like dropping a 155 mm howitzer round on an Al Qaeda stronghold. Poetry!

And depending on the types of folks you're playing with, never use a five-wood or iron where a driver is called for…unless they're accountants. Then you can talk about low risk, conservative strategies. *"Keep it safe...that's my motto."* Otherwise, if you want to use golf as a business tool, get good with the big stick. *"Man...you crushed that one!"*

There is an entire industry devoted to playing golf for business purposes. And there are many ways to use this great sport to bond with clients and prospects that go beyond the traditional eighteen holes and a beer. Go to www.golfforcause.com and learn more.

*Referral Strategy #10*

# Use A Referral Guide

## Concept overview:

- HNW clients and centers of influence want to know that you take referrals very seriously, and that when they give you a name of a client, friend or colleague, you are going to treat that person with extreme care and professionalism.

- Using a Referral Guide is a psychological positioning tool that sends all those messages.

- A Referral Guide allows you to expand your client's story-telling ability beyond a two-sentence conversation fragment.

- Developing a Referral Guide takes work and creativity. Because of that, it will help you stand above the competition.

It's time to combine many of our core referral principles into one tangible idea that is simple, inexpensive, and massively powerful for your success.

In basic form, a Referral Guide is a nothing more than a three-ring binder or a pocket folder. You're going to put stuff in it and you need to have the words Referral Guide somewhere on the front cover. That's it...you don't need to make it any more complicated. Advisors always ask me for a sample Referral Guide and my question is, *"Have you ever seen a three-ring binder? Then get one of those and you're all set."* The desire to make things more complex than necessary runs deep.

A three-ring binder is better than a pocket folder for a few reasons. Folders are cheap and more easily trashed or dumped in a drawer. Binders on the other hand generally have a very long shelf life and are stored somewhere visible like on a bookshelf. I still have my CFA exam study guides on a shelf in my office from more than five years ago. I have my Series 7 training materials from over two decades ago in my storage room. Of course those binders along with all my "papers" will eventually become part of the Maselli Memorial Library on the second floor of the Voorleezer's House at the Richmondtown Restoration on Staten Island...so they're destined for posterity.

Binders are also easy to add things to. You should actually plan to update your binder periodically when you visit the client. That's a great way to create a new referral conversation as well. Folders are easy to add to, but are taken less seriously than binders. There's just something about an item that's three-hole-punched that says, *"Take me seriously!"*

The Referral Guide is **not** your team marketing brochure. It is a stand-alone kit that deals specifically with the subject of referrals. If you have any marketing material, the Referral Guide should probably have a similar look and feel to it just to keep all your materials consistent. Your marketing brochure is actually one of the things that can go into the Referral Guide, so they should complement and support each other.

## Why use a Referral Guide?

Because the way you ask for the referral or bring up the subject of referrals with a top client or a center of influence will demonstrate the importance of referrals to you.

If you ask in a haphazard, unprepared, casual manner...that's how the client will assume you *handle* the referrals once they give you the name of a friend or colleague. So you cannot ask in an off-the-cuff or "Oh, by the way..." manner and expect a top client to believe that you really do treat them very seriously.

Therefore, the basic purpose of the Referral Guide is to upgrade or elevate the process of asking for referrals. It demonstrates that referrals are so important to you that you actually took the time to prepare an entire binder on the subject.

Remember the fear thing. Many HNW clients are terrified of giving you referrals for all the reasons that we've covered in this book. You must calm as much of that fear as you can...so I suggest you ask in a very serious, professional manner. The guide makes that possible better than anything I've used or seen.

## A branding statement

We talked earlier about branding. We said that the referral moment often comes down to a single conversation fragment of one or two sentences during which your client is going to try to tell your story to their friend.

Well that may not be enough for the HNW friend to make a decision. So now the client has something to fall back on. The guide becomes a tool they can use to tell your story. Or better yet, they can actually hand it to their friend and say, *"You should take a look at this...these guys are amazing!"*

The binder becomes your tangible presence in their office or home — your physical and spiritual link to their world. Every time they see it they're going to think of you and the referral process. It is a remarkably simple yet powerful ally...so use it!

## How to use the guide

The best way to use your Referral Guide is in a face-to-face meeting with a top client over dinner or lunch. You need to have a little uninterrupted time. At this meeting you are going to bring out the guide and actually walk them through it item by item at a reasonable but deliberate pace.

In doing so, you're trying to create the impression that you take referrals very seriously and you've given the whole subject lots of careful thought. In fact, this is true! The act of putting together a guide takes significant work. So this is one of those rare times when reality and perception coincide to leave a client with a strong, favorable assessment of your professionalism.

## What will the client do with the guide?

Three possibilities: first, they may refer back to it periodically when thinking about referring you to someone. Second, they may actually give it to someone they want to refer to you. In this way, the guide actually has two audiences, so you need to create it with that in mind, but your primary target is the existing client.

What's more likely, however, is that the client will stick the guide on a shelf and never look at it after that initial meeting. That's OK...it will still have done its job!

It's a message transmitter or a mind-state creator. It will have generated an amazing image in the client's head that will stay forever or until you screw it up by doing something dumb. Once the guide has done that critical job, everything else is gravy, so don't worry too much about its future use. In truth, you are building this guide mainly to facilitate a ten-minute referral conversation that will last a lifetime.

## *What goes in the guide?*

You can put almost anything you want in the guide, but there are a few items that you should definitely include. In general, I would avoid making it too bulky or cumbersome. Limit yourself to six to ten items at most so you can effectively walk the client through it in a single sitting without their eyes glazing over.

Ideally the items you include should all fit neatly inside and actually look like they belong together. They should be professionally crafted without looking like they were created by your firm's marketing department. Make fresh copies. Use color. Personalize everything that speaks to the client. Remember, you're only going to be making ten or fifteen of these guides for your best clients so spend the time and effort to do them right.

Here's a description of suggested items to include in your guide. Each would be a tab in the binder. You may add or subtract as you see fit.

## Referral Guide Tabs

| | |
|---|---|
| Introductory letter to the client | Team marketing brochure |
| Sample newsletters | Letters to the referral from you |
| Articles you have written | Referral questionnaire |
| Articles written about you | Ideal client profile |
| List of services | Center of Influence client profile |
| Calendar of events | Extra business cards (supplies) |
| Team Biography | Prizes! (optional) |

## 1. Introductory letter to the client

This is a personalized, one-page letter that explains the overall philosophy of referrals and addresses the two biggest fears the client has about the referral process. You are going to be talking through much of this philosophy, but the letter is a hard-copy reminder of what you said with some augmentations built in for future reference.

Here's an example of a letter I might use:

*Dear Bob,*

*I'm writing to thank you for allowing the Maselli Group to manage your investment and financial portfolio. We appreciate the trust you've placed in us and we are eager to help you reach your financial goals.*

*As you know, the investment world today can be complex and confusing. Recently, my partners and I have become very concerned that there are many investors out there who may not be getting the kind of quality attention and personal guidance they need. In that light, we have decided to open our practice to the personal referrals of our top clients.*

*As one of those top clients, our commitment to you extends to anyone in your world about whom you care deeply. That might include family members, friends or colleagues. Within that broad circle, it's possible that you may know someone who would appreciate our kind of personalized service or benefit from some of our insights concerning their investments. If that's true, you should know two things:*

*First, my team and I treat all referrals with the utmost care and discretion. Your referrals will receive the very best service and personalized attention. Their experience with the Maselli Group will be positive, highly professional and will reflect very well upon you.*

*Second, we maintain a strict policy of complete confidentiality. At no time will I or anyone on my staff discuss your portfolio or financial situation with anyone.*

*It may seem unnecessary to state these points so directly, but we value your referrals a great deal and I want you to know how seriously we take them. They are, in fact, the only way we accept new clients.*

*Again, thank you for the opportunity to be of service. We look forward to working with you.*

*Sincerely,*

*Frank Maselli*

This letter is simply a mini-form of the Strength Referral we discussed earlier. It also addresses the two big fears of embarrassment and confidentiality.

## 2. Sample newsletters

I love newsletters! We've already talked about this idea, but to me they are one of the simplest and most impactful tools you can use in your practice. Ideally you are able to write your own, but in lieu of that a firm-created piece is fine. Put one or two past issues of your newsletter in the guide. If you're not using a newsletter now I urge you to examine that strategy. You are competing with other advisors who do...and you're eventually going to lose that battle.

## 3. Articles you've written

This is similar to a newsletter only better! If you can write articles or have access to ghostwritten ones, you should think about this as part of your overall marketing strategy. People who write stuff are smart, important, and serious members of their profession who command respect and authority beyond the average competitor. Obviously that's one of my core life beliefs. You're free to disagree of course....but just who the hell are *you*? I wrote the damn book!

So write stuff.

*But what about compliance?*

Writing is absolutely not illegal folks. There is no NYSE or NASD regulation that says a registered rep cannot write articles or newsletters. I know scores of advisors who do this. Everything must be approved, of course, and you can't make outrageous claims just like any form of industry advertising, but they *can* be done.

Your firm may have its own policies about this, and there is probably a process in place to get written materials compliance approved. So while it may take effort to get your materials through compliance. The long-term benefit to your career is potentially enormous.

## 4. Articles written about you

One of the other great things you can do for your business is to get some ink about you and your team — preferably something other than mention in the local police blotter.

There are a number of ways to get the right kind of press on yourself and your team. You can cultivate a relationship with a reporter for a local paper. Reporters need stories. It's a tough job to come up with something to say every day and many would welcome help in doing a good story. Not that they want you to write it for them, but they would love an interesting idea with a clever angle they can sink their teeth into.

One challenge I've found with reporters is that many of them are looking for controversy. They will dig it out and stir it up every chance they get. Some have even been known to make it up entirely. Don't be shocked or take this personally...it's their job. Just be prepared.

You may think you've made a friend and that they are writing a nice "puff piece" about you and your team only to find out that you're part of an "in-depth expose" on the underbelly of the financial planning world. Now your casual mention of a golf outing with the wholesaler from XYZ Funds comes back with a new headline: **"Local Broker Admits to Resort Trips and Bribes!"**

Your quotes may be taken out of context. Your words will be re-fitted to new questions and the article that was supposed to help you get business may put you *out* of business. Can you tell that I've had some bad experiences with the press? Because of that I decided to get some quality training in this area and I suggest you do the same if you intend to work with the media in any form.

Not all reporters are like this, but ironically, the good ones often are. They have careers going too. And you don't win a Pulitzer by writing feel-good articles that are little more than ad copy for some local business owner. So tread intelligently and carefully and treat them with respect.

It might be better to develop an expertise in an area and then offer yourself for interviews on subjects that deal with those issues. Now you're a source and someone they can go to for background on a story. You might be able to help them get the right information or steer them in a certain direction on a subject they're not familiar with. This is all part of the relationship equation. It's a give and take and over time you might make a good friend with an intelligent, creative, and insightful professional — nothing wrong with that.

A parallel track is to hire a PR agent who can get you placed properly and help generate the kind of press you want. The issue here is cost and time. PR agents are not cheap. Many work on retainer so be prepared to spend several thousand dollars minimum on this effort.

Beyond the money, it takes work and thought. A good PR agent will want to get to know your business and the "hooks" that make it easier to sell a story about you to their press contacts. They are going to ask you questions about what you do and what makes you special. All of this is good for you and the process might actually help you refine your story, but it's not like you hire a PR agent and bam!...Suddenly you're on the cover of *Barron's* as "Top Advisor in America."

A good PR person might help you target publications that you might not normally consider for press. Several years ago I introduced one of my brokers to a PR agent who got him written up in a woman's magazine as one of the top advisors handling financial issues for divorced woman. We would never have thought of this, but it turned out to be such a goldmine for him that we had to install his own 800 line to handle the call volume!

## 5. List of services

Why give a client a list of services? Don't they already know what you do?

Ha! Most clients probably know less than 10% of what you are capable of. They think that what you do all day is what you did with them. Their perception is a very narrow slice of your total pie. Many times, they are hesitant to refer you because they think their friends would not need the same advice or investment programs you gave them. So show them the whole spectrum of what you do. This will help you cast a broader net for potential referrals.

On your List of Services you might want to include three sections:

### Things you specialize in:

These are the main areas on which you have chosen to focus your practice. Don't assume that the client knows any part of this list. For example, you may have done managed money with a top client. But they may not even be aware of the fact that you also do municipal bonds, mutual funds, or covered call writing. To the average client, these are alien concepts that sound totally different. We know them as normal parts of the typical investment practice, but the client knows NOTHING! Even the most sophisticated investors understand very little of our world. So spell it out in clear terms...which also means avoiding jargon like "equities and fixed-income securities." Instead say "stocks and bonds."

### Things your firm can do:

This is probably a big list so you might have to cut it back or categorize it a bit. If you work for a major financial services firm, try to highlight those areas that you think would be appealing to the clients you are targeting. I like to include things like 401(k)s; business lending; stock option financing; concentrated stock hedging; oil, gas and other commodities; and international investments. I want the client to know that I am part of a big world and that I can access that massive intelligence on behalf of their more sophisticated friends and contacts.

### Things you can refer a client to:

This is your network of other professionals that a top client may need. Obviously you can refer me to a great accountant or estate attorney. You should have several names ready to go at all times. Who else might you need on this list? Depending on your market you can include a whole host of ancillary professional services from aircraft loans to golf pros to hospice care providers.

## 6. Calendar of events

As we discussed earlier, holding events for your clients is a tremendous way to boost referrals. So in the kit, you want to include a complete listing of dates, times and locations of all the events you have planned for the year and beyond. I always like to throw in one or two things that are at least a year or two down the road.

A calendar like this not only gives people time to prepare, but it also sends a few positive subliminal messages about you.

First — you're organized. You plan things in advance and think them through...which are good characteristics.

Second — you're going to be here for the long haul. You are part of the community and plan to be part of your clients' lives for many years to come.

Third — you are a busy professional. You have lots of activities going on and plan months if not years in advance. I hope this is true.

## 7. Team biography or marketing brochure

You may already have this, if not, you should develop one soon. Of course, everyone on your team gets a bio. You may also want to include people who you may not normally think of as part of your team. Some examples I use are business coaches, great wholesalers who bring value to your business, your managers, and other professionals who regularly work with your clients. This is where you get to create a "virtual" team of specialists and experts who can be brought in on certain cases to solve problems. The goal is to let the client know that you are ready and able to address a broad array of their potential needs.

## 8. Intro letter to the referral from you

This would be a sample letter that you would send a referral when a client gives you a name. You show this letter to the client as a way of relaxing them about your approach. Here is a letter I might use:

*Dear Referral,*

*You have probably never heard of The Maselli Group, but one of our top clients and a mutual friend suggested that I drop you a line. Bob Smith of Allied Chemical thought that you might be intrigued by some of the unique services and ideas we have developed for use with executives such as yourself.*

A simple opening that tells the referral where you got his name and piques his curiosity with the words "intrigued" and "unique services.".

*We've worked with Bob for several years and built a great relationship of trust with him and his family over that time. Our practice is very selective and we work only by referral with a small handful of top executives in the community. Bob is one of our favorite people and he thinks very highly of you...so I am writing to introduce myself.*

Give a little history about you and Bob, but obviously no investment details. This could be tweaked for a different kind of referral such as a corporate account or a 401(k).

*I would enjoy a chance to talk with you about some of the things we can do at the Maselli Group and how those strategies might positively impact your financial and investment needs today or potentially down the road.*

*Bob also mentioned that you enjoy an occasional round of golf. I'd like to invite you to join me at the Franklin Country Club on Wednesday the 12th or Saturday the 15th of June if those dates work. If not, we may be able to flex around your schedule. I will call your office later this week to touch base.*

This is the action step. This paragraph can be switched out with others as the specific circumstances apply.

*Best regards,*

*Frank Maselli*

The body of this letter would remain fairly constant, but I might change the action step depending on the circumstances of the case. For example, this might be an alternative ending.

*Bob also mentioned that you might enjoy attending one of our Strategic Insight dinners at the Capital Grill. Our next event is on June 23rd at 7:00 and will feature a portfolio manager for one of the top money management firms in the industry. This might give us a chance to chat and for you to see a bit more about what we do here at Maselli Group. These are usually very enjoyable and insightful events. I'm sure Bob can tell you more about them.*

*I will call your office later this week to touch base.*

You might want to include two or three letters in your Referral Guide, each with a slightly different ending, and let the client choose the one he feels most comfortable with.

## 9. Referral questionnaire

Fill out with the help of the referring client. The goal is to capture as much information as possible about the referral before the initial contact. Some clients may be reluctant to reveal too much information about a friend...so be relaxed. This isn't the Spanish Inquisition. Get whatever you can and be happy. Here's a sample referral questionnaire:

# Referral Questionnaire

| Name | Age | Spouse's Name | Age |
|------|-----|---------------|-----|

**Address**

| Phone 1 | Children ☐YES ☐NO<br>Names and ages |
|---------|------|
| Phone 2 | |
| E-mail | Grandchildren ☐YES ☐NO<br>Names and ages |
| Preferred contact method | Investment experience or information |
| Client's relationship to referral | |

| Company | Years there | Retirement plan?<br>☐DB ☐DC ☐_____ |
|---------|-------------|-----------------|

Title, position or responsibilities

Notes

## 10. The ideal client profile

This is a one-pager you would prepare to let the client know the kinds of prospective referrals you are looking for. You can make it broad and general or narrow and detailed depending on the type of practice you're trying to build or message you want to send to that specific client.

For example, if you're giving this to a business owner, you might want to focus on entrepreneurs or other people he is most likely to know. So maybe you keep 80% of it the same and only customize 20% for the client. That would be enough for you to rationalize not sending it back through compliance each time you use it.

I'm not going to give you a sample of this profile because I personally wouldn't use the one I just described to you. Mine is probably not going to satisfy your need for complexity, detail, and over-thinking. My Ideal Client Profile is much simpler and is designed to uncover the exact type of client I truly love.

> *At the Maselli Group, we work with investors who care deeply about the important things in life and who find joy in places far more permanent than beating the S&P 500, achieving a lower portfolio standard deviation, or being invested in the hot asset class of the week.*
>
> *We work with those investors who realize that navigating this ocean of noise and confusion on the way to a more secure and enjoyable life is a difficult journey that will require discipline, patience and planning...but that given those attributes, along with a sense of irony and humor...we will most assuredly get there and have fun along the way.*
>
> *We work with investors who understand that tomorrow is always brighter and that the markets, while temporarily out of balance, are ultimately a measure of the unlimited human spirit. They seek to participate in that incredible experience over multiple lifetimes for themselves and their progeny.*
>
> *Finally we work with people who recognize the value in using professional, skilled, trained, and caring*

*advisors to guide them on that journey and who are willing to pay a fair price for that help.*

*If you know anyone like this...we would be pleased to talk with them.*

Works for me.

## 11. Center of Influence ideal client profile

This is a page you fill out for each of your partner CPAs, attorneys and other professionals to find out who *their* ideal clients may be. As a document, it's very simple — basically a blank note sheet with the words "Bob's Ideal Clients" written on top. You will use it in an interview with the CPA to learn about their practice.

There has always been an unspoken *quid pro quo* between several related professions in the financial field – you give me referrals...I give you referrals. That arrangement works well and is beneficial to all parties. What you are doing with this profile is taking that informal agreement and making it more official and professional. I might say something like this:

*Jack (the CPA), we are obviously in a position to help each other here. I have clients who will need accounting help at some point and I would like to be able to refer them to you. Take a few minutes and tell me a little about your practice. What kinds of clients are you looking for and how can I help you find them?*

This interview process will elevate your stature in the mind of the CPA or center of influence in a very meaningful way. It lets them know that you are a careful professional who takes referrals very seriously and that you are real partner who is genuinely interested in their success as well as your own. It's a two way street.

You can also use this interview idea with a wide array of folks beyond the traditional referral sources you may have considered. Think about all the professionals who deal with HNW clients in some way. Find the ones who work with the kinds of clients you might like and who could also benefit from referrals from you. This must be a viable two-way street.

This list can include people from what I call the "service professions" such as accountants, attorneys, business managers, sports or theatrical agents, insurance agents, etc.

Then take a look at the "lifestyle professions" such as golf and tennis pros, restaurant owners, personal trainers, boat and airplane brokers, car sales people, stable owners, dog breeders, hunting and fishing guides, clothing salespeople, home contractors, travel agents. The list goes on.

These lifestyle folks may not be as close to the actual finances as the service people but they do occupy a position of trust in the life of your potential referral.

Think creatively and keep your eyes open for opportunities to link up with other top professionals with whom you can share ideas and services. After they prove themselves to be reliable, you might add them to your "virtual team" and make them part of your overall service model.

## 12. Supplies

Be sure you to include a small supply of business cards in your Referral Guide. That may seem too trivial to mention, but it's not. And don't just stuff them in the side pocket...put them in a nice card case or holder that keeps them neat and looking professional. When the moment comes for your client to refer you to a friend, there's nothing worse than having them hand out a chewed up, dirty business car with the corners all bent. Well, there is *one* thing worse and that no card at all! So make it easy for the client to share your name with a friend.

## 13. Prizes

*What?* Yes...I said prizes...as in gifts to clients for referrals.

*Do you mean put a list of prizes in my referral guide?*

Yes...but let me tell a quick story first.

I worked with an top advisor once who used to send out a quarterly newsletter to his clients. It was nothing fancy...just a simple, 2-page piece consisting mainly of regurgitated commentary from our firm's analysts and economists. In truth, you probably couldn't get something like this past compliance today, but that's beside the point.

On the front page of his newsletter, he had a special boxed section called **"The Referral Club."** In this box you would read things like…

*"Congratulations to Joe and Donna. They made it to the Gold Level referral club. They win a dinner for two at Rex!"*

Rex was this fancy restaurant in Los Angeles where they filmed the snail scene in the movie *Pretty Woman*. Stanley could get you a great table at Rex on the busiest night of the week. They always made room when he called because he was a player. Did I mention that he was doing about three million in gross back in the 1980s and early 90s when that was real money.

In that newsletter you might also read something like…

*"Congratulations to Len and Susan…they made it to the Platinum Level Referral Club. They win a weekend for two at La Costa Spa."*

Now I am not recommending a spa weekend for your top clients…or am I? Wait…it gets better.

So one day I'm walking around the office doing my manager thing and I see Stanley waiving his arms for me to come over. I see the phone line is blinking on his desk and he says, *"Listen to this…you're gonna get a kick out of it!"*

He punches up the line on the speaker phone and this is what I hear with my own ears…

*"Stanley…its Dr. Morris. How are you?"*

*"Great Doc…how are you?"*

Now I know Dr. Morris. He's one of Stanley's biggest clients. A plastic surgeon in Beverly Hills…huge money!

*"Stanley…I just got this little newsletter of yours and I was wondering…JUST HOW DOES SOMEONE GET TO THE GOLD LEVEL REFERRAL CLUB?"*

Dr. Morris, the whale, took the bait. This was the magic moment. So what does a total genius say at this point?

*"Give me ten names and you're in."*

*"Whatever you feel like Doc."*

*"Just refer someone like you."*

No...none of the above. Those are for amateurs. Here's a genius at work.

*"Doc...I've gotta' be honest. You have no shot for gold. Why don't you just try for silver instead?"*

Bamn...the epiphany moment. Lightening struck. Why was that genius? Stanley knew his client. Remember Rule 405...Know Your Client — as if there are 404 rules more important than that.

Stanley knew that this guy was a big dog — a plastic surgeon in Beverly Hills for Pete's sake! He's not used to hearing the words, *"I'm sorry you don't qualify for gold status."* So in a moment of sheer brilliance, he took it away from him. It was a gamble, like a Texas Hold'Em player going all-in. I was stunned...and then over the speaker I heard a different tone of voice...

*"Stanley...you listen to me. Go to your fax machine. I am sending you the name of every surgeon in my building. You tell them I said to call. I WANT THAT DINNER FOR TWO...DO WE UNDERSTAND EACH OTHER?"*

Could this guy afford his own dinner for two? Of course! Yet he was willing to throw all his friends under a bus for a dinner for two!

I stood there in awe as Stanley hung up the phone. I think even he was surprised by the words that burst out of his mouth at that magic moment. I doubt he had planned this strategy. More like a lion hunting a wounded gazelle...he was reacting on instinct...and the neck was snapped! Ninety seconds later here comes the fax...14 pages of doctors, pictures, profiles, specialties, addresses and phone numbers.

Now this story has nothing to do with my recommended referral strategies. I don't think today's HNW clients would risk their deepest personal relationships for gifts of dinners or spa trips. Even if you could afford it...is that the right way to build your business?

The answer is maybe. Stanley didn't want Dr. Morris' deepest relationships. He wanted a few names and permission to say, *"Dr. Morris suggested that I call you."* That was not the same level of referral we are seeking with my strategies. I only tell this story as an example of the amazingly broad range of possibilities that you face every day in your interactions with HNW clients. Stanley was a master salesman. His skills were from an earlier era and they worked for his time. Some of his skills, however, were timeless….chief among those were people skills.

The instinct for knowing what drives people never goes out of style. So just keep your eyes and ears open and trust your gut. Don't close the door on an *easy* referral just because it's supposed to be hard. You never know when you will run into someone who just wants to impress you or feel like an important player in your eyes for whatever personal reasons they may have. Let them enjoy themselves and be happy.

Sometimes luck is better than brains. Frankly, If you have the kind of client relationships where they bring you a steady stream of qualified referrals and all you have to do is set up a few trips, events, outings, dinners or excursions like these…I would do that every day and twice on Sunday's! That would be very unlikely…but if it works for you than you are among the blessed, so cross your fingers and keep going.

That's it for the Referral Guide. You can add or subtract items as you see fit. Keep it simple enough to walk the client through it in a single setting. If you make it too complex or thick…it's going in the drawer never to see the light of day.

---

## The Referral Guide®

1.  Introductory letter that explains your referral process
2.  Sample newsletters
3.  Articles you've written
4.  Articles written about you
5.  List of services (you, the firm, your network))
6.  Calendar of events
7.  Team biography or marketing brochure
8.  Letters to the referral from you (two or three samples)
9.  Referral questionnaire
10. Ideal client profile
11. Center of Influence ideal client profile
12. Supplies (extra cards in a case)
13. Prizes *(*optional)*

## *Using the guide on day one*

Firsts are a big deal. First date, first kiss, first day on the job, first child, first million...whatever. The first of anything carries added emotional weight. First day with a new client is just as important and what you do during that interaction will long be remembered. It may actually color the entire relationship for years to come.

Asking a brand new HNW client for referrals may be one of the most uniquely awkward moments in all of sales. So don't do it!

Instead, bring up the subject of referrals in a professional manner that speeds up the trust-building process. Doing so creates a positive referral mind-state that should last the length of the relationship.

We've been taught to ask for referrals right away, and I think I've shown that this is a wrong-headed approach. The new client is only at Level One Trust and this insane acceleration to Level Three may leave them with emotional whiplash!

But you are certain that this client knows other people who need your help. So you want to plant very strong referral seeds in their mind right away in hopes of harvesting some great new relationships as soon as possible. Let's learn how to do this.

## *The Sign-Aboard Meeting*

This is the meeting where the prospect actually becomes a client. They sign the check, the transfer form or the new account form and they hand everything to you. This is the magic moment that officially makes them "clients." This is a dangerous moment for several reasons.

Any person who has ever made a major buying decision like a new car or a house knows the power and fear of this moment. Some call it "buyer's remorse." It's actually a complex set of psychological processes that come together to create tension and stress in the mind of many people. It must be handled with extreme care and sensitivity otherwise you run enormous risks.

You can bring up the subject of referrals now, but do it without asking. That's a subtle but important difference in approach. Here's how it might go.

## The Transition phrase

This is where you smooth over the sign-aboard moment with a gentle, friendly message of welcome. Pick a few and mix them up:

*I'm very happy to have you on board!*

*I think you're going to like the way we do things at The Maselli Group.*

*I think you're going to look back on this moment as a really good decision for your family and your future.*

*I'm excited to get started together!*

*It's going to be fun working with you.*

*Welcome to the team.*

*Congratulations...you've made a great decision.*

There are a hundred potential things you can say here but the purpose of saying anything is simply to smooth over the emotional bump in the road and begin to transition to the next phase of the conversation.

You continue...

*Bob before we wrap up, I want to give you something that's very important to us, and it will probably become very important to you too as we move forward together. It has to do with our professional mission at the Maselli Group.*

*You may have noticed how screwed up and confused the world of finance feels today. There's a tremendous amount of conflicting advice and noise coming from all sides. A lot of folks are very scared and bewildered about their money.*

*It's possible that you may know someone now or down the road — a friend or family member that might need financial help at some point. If that happens, you need to know that our commitment to you extends to anyone in your world that you care deeply about. Now that you are part of the Maselli Group, our services are available to you and your family and friends at any time.*

*Hey...it's our first day together. You don't even know what we are capable of yet. You took a leap of faith here today...I realize that and I appreciate the trust you've shown.*

*But over time you are going to see that we really are quite good at what we do. I want you to know that this process, this discipline, our ideas, our full financial arsenal is open to the people in your world.*

There it is again — the Strength Referral. It's not about building your business...it's about helping the people they care most about....which I hasten to remind you is absolutely 100% true and accurate. Now that Bob is a client he has access to an entire spectrum of incredible financial advice. He gets the pass code and the secret handshake that admits him into the rarified world of you. And he gets to bring friends!

Now you cement your professionalism with the Referral Guide.

*Take this with you. It's our Referral Guide. It will tell you everything about how we handle the people in your world who might need our help*

*There are some specific things we do with referrals and they work very well. We take referrals very seriously as you might imagine. This is not a hobby for us...it's a science and our clients appreciate the way we handle their friends.*

*Our team mission is to help people, but we can't help everyone so we have to be selective. We have a unique practice and we want to keep it that way. The only way we accept new clients is through referrals from existing clients. It's just a decision we've made to offer our services first to the people who understand and appreciate the kind of work we do.*

*Let me walk you through this for a minute just so you know what's in here.*

Bamn...you're done! You've brought up referrals in a very professional and different way. You've started on day one with a brand new client to create the referrals only practice. You did it with total honesty and care for this person who has entrusted at least a part of his wealth to you. You're on your way.

# Next Steps

This is a lot of information to digest. So what should you do with all these strategies? The answer will depend on where you are today in your business, but let me give you a set of possible next steps that will get you started on the road to professional referrals. First...a reminder:

## The 10 Strategies:

1. Develop a referral plan
2. Provide excellent service
3. Position referrals from strength
4. Stay top-of-mind
5. Address the risks and emotions of referrals
6. Target a specific industry or client niche
7. Tell your story boldly
8. Use the New Specialty Referral
9. Use the Event Referral
10. Use a Referral Guide

The following outline of next steps is roughly in chronological order but you may be at different stages for various parts of the referral process. Also, several can be occurring simultaneously...so you may have a few activities from different phases going on at once, which is normal.

However you proceed, do something! Don't let this book become a mere academic discussion. Goal-directed activity is the key to success. You now know what to do...so get started today!

## *Your referral to-do list*

1.  Decide who you are and what makes you referable
    a.  Assess the trust levels (1-2-3) of your current relationships
    b.  Why would your top clients want to refer you?
    c.  Why might they NOT want to refer you?
2.  Begin building your branding story so that you have a message to deliver
    a.  Assess your team's greatest strengths
    b.  Take the Kolbe A Index and get an evaluation
    c.  Take the Financial DNA Path Profiles
    d.  Develop your team's Core Principles
3.  Start building you Referral Plan
    a.  List twenty clients and COIs you want referrals from
    b.  List twenty prospects you want to be referred to
    c.  Begin gathering data for your Referral Intelligence File
        o   personal world
        o   professional world
        o   community
        o   specific names of potential referrals or client links
4.  Conduct a service quality assessment
    a.  Start with an internal analysis of strengths and struggles
    b.  Ask selected top clients for their evaluation
    c.  Begin corrective action if necessary
5.  Decide what you will do to stay top-of-mind with your best clients
    a.  Implement the Forty-Four Touch System
    b.  Start using a newsletter
    c.  send magazine subscriptions to your top twenty clients
6.  Examine potential niche client groups or industries to target
    a.  List the top industries in your community or marketing area
    b.  List your favorite clients and their industries
    c.  Look for overlap, what is your penetration of these top industries?

    d.   Look for potential industry clusters among your favorite groups

7.   Develop a new business specialty

8.   Develop a calendar of possible referral events you can plan for the year

9.   Begin building your Referral Guide

    a.   Start with the basic list of items as outlined in Strategy #10

    b.   Decide which Centers of Influence you are going to approach

    c.   Get some press coverage and have articles written about you for the kit

    d.   Write your own articles for the kit

10.  Meet with your clients and use the Strength Referral Message

11.  Have some fun!

That's a good basic list of next steps and it should keep you busy for the year if you commit to making referrals a serious part of your world. Don't over-complicate this process. You have learned the critical steps and while they take some work…they are not rocket science. Even a raw rookie can get started on this program today!

# Final Thoughts

You now have a few things to think about. These Ten Strategies will help you increase your referrals if you use them. But *that's* the part I cannot control. Only you can determine what you will and will not do at any moment. You will be guided by your new skills, driven by your instinctive strengths and powered by your desire to help people and achieve personal success. Failure is not in your future.

I just want to leave you with one last thought...and don't take this the wrong way please. This is not a negative message although it may sound like that at first.

In my travels, I talk with thousands of advisors every year. I am in a unique position to view nearly the full range of the financial advisory profession. I've personally worked with teams that rank in the top ten in the entire industry as well as with brand new rookies who could barely find the way to the restrooms. I've worked with sole-practitioner planners who operate from their basements as well as fifty-year wirehouse veterans in corner offices in Manhattan.

I've learned that this business is not for everyone. It's a very tough journey that demands a lot of you both intellectually and emotionally. Physically, thank goodness it's easy or I'd be screwed, but my point is that success in this industry takes a certain breed of person. Not a *better* person — just someone with slightly different internal wiring than the average human being out there walking around. Something drew you into this business and then something else compelled you to read this book, so I'm guessing you are that kind of person.

Here's my message...

This industry is about to undergo a massive shakeout. It has happened before and I think it's coming again. Over the next few years, we may see a significant reduction of the number of financial advisors. It's possible that as many as one-half will be gone over the next ten years! And if not gone then probably on a salary of some kind.

The evolutionary process in our industry is going to spawn new opportunities and new species of advisors...but only for the fittest of us. So I am asking you to take a very hard look at yourself and make a committed decision to evolve and hang on!  Do not be on that departing bus.

Many changes are already underway and many advisors are waking up to see their world transformed. I'm not saying that change is bad...quite the opposite. Success will be found at every level of the industry in some form. Just make sure whatever happens to you is by your own conscious choice...not someone else's.

To insure self-determination, you may need to boost the intensity and quality of your efforts. That may mean working harder, smarter, learning new skills, studying, reading, getting help from a coach, developing a specialty, opening the office on weekends, being more assertive, listening to tapes, going to seminars...whatever!

Do what you must and get started today to adapt yourself and your business to the new industry model. Once the shakeout phase is over you will be very glad you stayed on the team.

Folks...right now you are starting players in the greatest game man has ever invented. Give yourself every opportunity to be the best you can be and to reap the joy and rewards that your skills and passion merit.

And always remember that this is a people business. Money and investing may be the backdrop, but the real heart of what we do every day is take great care of people. Master that and you're home!

I welcome your comments about this book. If you say something really nice we may include your kind words in the next printing. If you hated the book, you probably haven't read it this far anyway, so who cares? If you would like more info on our free IXIS Advisor Academy training programs...shoot me an e-mail at fmaselli@ixisag.com.

Finally, I wish you the best of luck! You're fighting a tough battle, but you are not alone. There are many bright and caring folks out here who are eager and ready to help you...so reach out.